LUCK HAS LITTLE TO DO WITH IT

TO DO WITH IT

SUGGESTIONS FOR SUCCESSFUL SMALL STREAM FLY FISHING

by *Corky Henson*

F. C. "CORKY" HENSON
FAMOUS BAMBOO ROD MAKER

ROBERT GOODWIN
FAMOUS WILDERNESS GUIDE

WATT MURRAH
FAMOUS TEXAS JUDGE

ISBN 978-1-937851-13-2

Library of Congress Control Number: 2013936703

Cover and Text Design: Steve Smith FluiDESIGNS

First Edition
Printed in the United States of America

Western Reflections Publishing Company™
P.O. Box 1149
951 N. Highway 149
Lake City, CO 81235
www. westernreflectionspublishing.com

LUCK HAS LITTLE TO DO WITH IT

TABLE OF CONTENTS

Introduction   The Role of Luck in Fishing Small Streams..v
Chapter One.   How to Use the Suggestions in this
                      Little Book of Wisdom. 1
Chapter Two.   Small Streams Are Different.........................5
Chapter Three.   Flies in the Stream Catch More Trout..........9
Chapter Four.   Stealth...13
Chapter Five.   Where's the Trout?....................................19
Chapter Six.   Casting Effectively....................................23
Chapter Seven.   Wakes, Slack and Natural Bugs...................35
Chapter Eight.   Situations and Strategies............................41
Chapter Nine.   The Last Foot: Landing That
                      Unexpected Large Trout.............................55
Chapter Ten .   Small Streams and Kids..............................59
Chapter Eleven.   Small Stream Trout and Their Habits..........65
Chapter Twelve.   Equipment..73
Chapter Thirteen.   On Stream Behavior and Etiquette.............79
Chapter Fourteen.   Where are these Wonderful
                      Small Streams?..83
Chapter Fifteen.   Conservation, Deceit and the
                      Responsible Angler....................................91
Chapter Sixteen.   A Final Word of Encouragement................93
Chapter Seventeen.   Where We Put It All Together.....................97

ACKNOWLEDGEMENTS

This book evolved over several years and included an intermediate step, a brief pamphlet which the authors dispensed to friends, family, and a few clients. We are grateful for their critical and encouraging comments leading to the present work.

The initiating events for even the earlier pamphlet were several. They included a number of fishing trips with anglers new or relatively new to small stream fishing. Observing our common problems of successfully entering this unique fishing domain and describing methods of doing so were clearly important to constructing and organizing our thoughts. Frequently conversations among the authors and with these special angling partners occurred at the end of the day "over the campfire," and were instructional as well as stimulating! We continue to appreciate the opportunity to fish and learn with these hardy souls.

A specific initiating event is of note: Ruben Chambers, a long time summer resident of South Fork, Colorado, and a legendary small stream fisherman, was approached a few years ago at a favorite stream and asked, "Any luck?" Mr. Chambers responded "Luck has little to do with it." as he indicated a very nice stringer of trout. Thus was born the title of this book and, more importantly, thoughts of how does one learn to fish more successfully on small streams. Thank you, Ruben.

Clearly a book of this nature would have little impact and be less than entertaining without pictures, and good ones, relevant to the subject and in color. While many of the images herein came from the authors' libraries, we also gratefully acknowledge the several contributions of Vicky Moore, an accomplished angler as well as photographer. She is pictured in Chapter Seven.

Watt Murrah would like to recognize and thank Roy B. Siler, who fly fished the Rocky Mountains for over sixty years, for introducing him to the joys of fly fishing. Roy fishes higher waters now but his nephew, Watt, never spends a day on the stream without remembering him fondly.

Finally and most importantly the authors wish to thank our spouses; Jean Henson, Peggy Goodwin and Jackie Murrah, for their patience with our fishing (and other) habits, the least of which includes breakfast at 5:00 a.m. and dinner at 9:00 p.m. just so we can spend more daylight on these special waters.

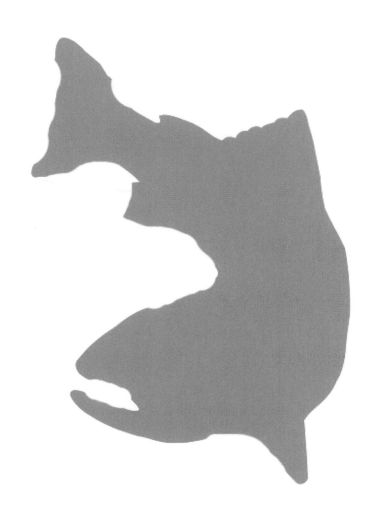

LUCK HAS LITTLE TO DO WITH IT

Introduction and the Role of Luck in Fly Fishing Small Streams

"I gotta admit that when I seen the four of a kind it looked to me like a hoss and a saddle, and a month of fishin' up the Crystal Mountains."
Harry Destry, in Destry Rides Again
Max Brand, 1930

Congratulations on buying this succinct book describing ways to improve your fishing success on small streams. And thanks for your confidence in us to deliver what we promise. Book introductions are, or should be, about intent, promises and background so that's what we'll try to address here.

The authors' purpose in writing this book is to help you have more fun as a small stream angler. Our definition of "fun"

is important to introduce at this point. We mean catch more fish; we mean catch the specific trout you target; we mean get past the tools so you can enjoy the experience; we mean share your skill and the small stream environment with other deserving anglers; we mean all of these. We propose to do that by sharing with you the most useful knowledge gleaned from the over 100 years of experience we collectively have around this most pleasurable pursuit— and to help keep you from having to learn mainly by mistakes. We've attempted to organize this experience in such a way that it is both useful and easily learned, hopefully leading you quickly to more success at fishing these delightful gems of the mountains. The book is itself organized in short, pithy chapters as we have resisted the temptation to pile in a bunch of words just to make it thicker and, perhaps, higher priced. This means you can refer to specific topics easily, as a continuing reference and reminder, after you've absorbed the entire book.

We promise these ideas, instruction and tips work, and they work best together. In all appropriate modesty, we are led to this promise by the fact that we generally catch more fish on small streams than do our friends and clients as we fish together.

At the same time it is important to realize, dear reader, that you have a most crucial role in this promised success. You must practice that which we suggest. If you make no change in your angling approach to small streams as a result of reading this book, our promise cannot be valid.

Most importantly, we hope our efforts here will be entertaining to you as well as adding to your angling skill set.

Now, we promised some comments on the role of luck in fly fishing small streams. The traditional question to the angler; "Have any luck today?" does have some relevance to success in small stream fishing, but, by definition, only by chance. (For a broader, perhaps dissenting, view, please read Chapter Seventeen – but not yet.)

"Luck" is defined in the dictionary as "a force that brings good fortune or adversity" and "lucky" is defined as "producing or resulting in good by chance." A force? You will note that this book is in the outdoor sports section of the book store, not the science fiction section alongside *Star Wars*! By chance? Well, that's different. Yes, chance can have (a little) something to do with catching fish; even trout! For example, anglers who ostensibly depend a great deal on luck or chance for their fishing success will almost always cast their fly to the water rather than to the land, thereby increasing their "chance" of catching a fish. Furthermore, they will select specific areas in the water in which to drop their fly, knowing that, at any given time, the fish present in that water are not randomly nor evenly distributed as to location. These anglers know the fish will be concentrated due to their need for food, protection or procreation. More experienced anglers do a great deal more than that in order to regularly catch fish. They fish successfully from experience; naturally, without much thought, and are probably pretty modest about their substantial skills on top of that! And that's what this book is all about: to explain the skills useful to increase the angler's chance of catching a fish and to help the angler become comfortable and natural applying those skills. The venue is the small stream; the fish is trout or char. But some of these suggestions might work elsewhere and on other fish as well.

Consistent success in fishing small streams is largely a matter of applying these skills; as we have demonstrated many times with friends and clients on the stream. (We will vouch for each other in this claim.) So, if you want to become a better fisherman; read, remember, and practice the following suggestions. If you do, we guarantee you'll catch more and larger fish from small streams. Now for those who feel luck has the greater part to play in your fishing success, no matter what the water, just skip ahead to our last chapter. You may find some small portion of vindication of your opinion and will then be well satisfied in the purchase of this book. We aim to please.

If you choose to read, even study, the whole book, and it's recommended that you do, you'll find plenty of tips on how to enhance your luck. Maybe to the extent that you, too, decide that luck has little to do with it.

It's also possible you will find yourself somewhat offended in reading some of the following chapters because the authors might take a dim view of one or more of your favorite fishing habits. These descriptions are not intended to be personal, but please know there is no intention of being politically correct here. There is more than enough of that elsewhere. Mother Nature is not politically correct and political correctness impedes factual learning by obscuring truth. The objective here is to identify, explain and illustrate as many of the best ways as we know to be successful fly fishing on small streams, and we want to do it in a high impact way. Our combined experience in this type fishing sums to more than 100 years spanning over four decades. Some of us have even read stuff on fishing published even before that. What we've learned by experience and by other means is the basis of the content of this book. In all honesty, all anglers are constantly learning, so we know that we are not the final authority. We therefore invite your new input to the next edition of this guide.

A part of what we do here is to point out what not to do as well as corrective or replacement behavior. Another part is to suggest ideas for success you may not have considered in the past. Both approaches offer substantial opportunities to have more fun fishing small streams for novice and advanced fly fishermen alike. And what else is angling about, anyway?

You may be surprised that many of the techniques discussed here are very basic; statements of the obvious, things you've heard or read somewhere else. After reading some of the ideas in this book, it's possible you'll say "I already knew that!" Well, "knowing it" and "doing it" can be two different things and the guarantee mentioned above is void if you don't learn to "do it." So part of our purpose here is to stimulate your desire to advance from the theoretical to the applied. Also, if there is any magic here, it's putting these ideas and suggestions together into a strategy or even habit as called for by the conditions you face on the stream. Therefore, in keeping with the "adult learning model," it is appropriate that you engage in candid self-analysis of your skill level, along with a corresponding commitment to change, if necessary. Also for maximum effectiveness you should practice these suggestions together as the fishing situation dictates, rather than just be aware of the individual bits of wisdom in a superficial fashion. The next chapter offers advice on how to combine these elements of success and make them an ongoing part of your fishing habits. If you still don't "get it" and choose not to "do it;" or if you insist on relying mostly on luck for your fishing success, and don't see a substantial increase in your small stream fishing success, it won't be our fault. You'll have to check the mirror for that. Or re-read the last chapter in this book – and be content.

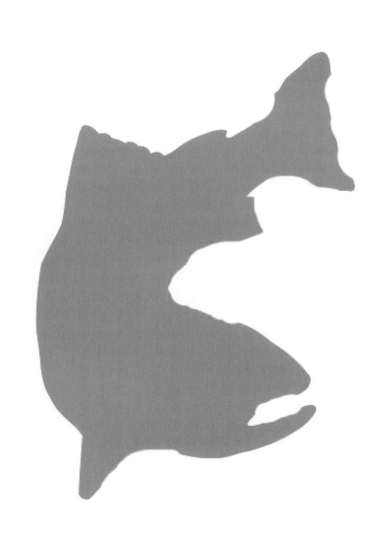

Chapter One
How to Use This Little Book of Wisdom

*"Never throw your fly, or put your bait into the water,
without expecting a fish."*
Hewett Wheately, Esq., The Rod and Line (1849)

The question is: "How can I use this book to improve my success in fishing on small streams?" The first seven chapters cover the basic considerations for success on small streams so one could quickly review these chapters to gain an initial sense of how to adapt to small stream fishing. Further details and specific guidance follow in the remaining chapters. Maybe that helps you get started or build on what you already know about fishing, but we don't think there's a real shortcut; it's gonna take some effort and practice to develop and improve the skills appropriate to small streams. If "effort and practice" sounds like fishing and fishing is fun to you, this should sound interesting and entertaining. If not, maybe you should return the book before you get bored with it and give us a bad review, or something.

Reading is one thing; learning is another. A suggested approach to integrating these great suggestions into your skill set (i.e., learning) follows: First, as you read the chapters and suggestions ahead, take time to reflect on your own related experience. If you've fished small streams before, picture how you addressed similar problems and the corresponding results. Would you do it differently having read and considered our suggestion? Imagine how you might utilize each of these suggestions on stream. Ask folks whose fishing talents you respect. What does he or she think about these suggestions? It's okay to write in the margins of this book, so make notes. Who knows; perhaps your grandchildren will enjoy reading them long after you're gone. The idea here is to build an image of success and confidence even before you have the opportunity to practice on stream. Some of these techniques can be practiced in your back yard or in the local park. Do so.

Use the checklist provided at the back of the book to remind you of appropriate considerations when you arrive at a good stream, and, most importantly, before you just start casting! Stop fishing after awhile; even if you are having a good day. Reflect a few minutes on where you're having fun and what you might do even better to catch more and larger fish. If the "fish aren't biting," STOP RIGHT NOW! A legally acceptable definition of insanity is to keep doing the same things but expect different results! Maybe it's time to refer to the checklist again while you drink some water or have a trail bar, or just sit in the shade a bit and enjoy the scenery. Find the one or two things you are not doing according to this fine and reliable advice. Change 'em and try again. You might have to do this a couple of times, but rest assured that our approach works! You can trust us as we are not, for the most part, politicians. But we do realize that there is an exception to our guarantee; the barren stream. It could be barren due to pollution, irresponsible fishing with worms, or perhaps it's too shallow to sustain a fish population through the winter at this particular altitude. It's really disappointing to find one of these streams, but it does happen.

At the end of the day reflect some on your success and the elements of that success; especially rerun in your mind how you caught the two or three biggest fish or the strike that surprised you or the best section of the stream, etc. In other words, remember the elements of your success so you can learn from them. You'll also have a better story for your friends this way. Enjoy their expressions and, perhaps, their envy. Then ask for their corresponding experience; don't pass up a chance to learn.

Some folks like to record their experience in a fishing diary. Try it. It'll help you catch fish the next time you fish a small stream, if you read it. It will also help you sort memories next winter, while you are planning your next trip.

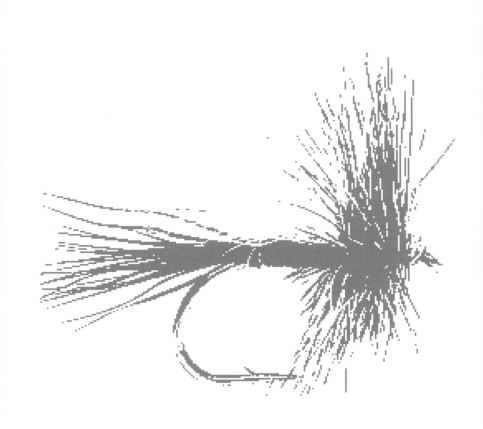

Chapter Two
Small Streams Are Different

"Coming to new water, you have to learn it afresh: each river has a strong individuality. I have known anglers, successful on one water they know well, fail utterly on another and what seemed to me less exacting stream. To be fully qualified, a fisherman must have fished widely and well as intensively: and the wider his experience the less is he inclined to generalize."

John Waller Hills, *A Summer on the Test* (1930)

Well, of course small streams are different; they're small, compact, little. The water is shallow and sometimes there are willows and other brush guarding what stream there is. A "deep pool" is three feet deep, not eight or ten feet deep. Your shadow will fall all the way across the stream, even in late morning or early afternoon. Most of these delightful waters are high in the mountains, very, very, clear and wonderfully cold. You're not in Kansas anymore, Toto!

We want to discuss the nature of small streams because we think an angler must adjust his or her attitude in order to really master the unique fishing offered by these waters. If you will be open to some new perspectives on small streams, we think we can help you move from the "just a Brookie stream" attitude to "I prefer the challenge of small mountain streams." And, yes, it's easy to catch little Brook Trout in most mountain streams, but there's a lot more to gain from a close relationship with small streams. The list includes large fish, wild fish, relatively rare fish, challenging fly presentation opportunities, awesome scenery, improved health, solitude.... And why do you fly fish???

Everything that happens in and around a small stream is bigger than in or around a large body of water, relatively speaking. Take a minute and think about what this statement means. Shallow water can change a critical few degrees in temperature more rapidly than you'd expect, changing fish feeding habits quickly, especially if the stream flows thru a nice, sunny meadow. If in a meadow, the ambient temperature, and thus the type of insects about, can change dramatically in a short time. Your observations related to fly selection can be out-of-date really fast. In just a few yards you might go from relatively quiet water to swift pocket water, and of course the resident fish act differently in those two environments. And how about the wind. A light breeze over a small stream might disturb its surface, which makes it harder to see the fish but it's also harder for them to see you, especially if you move slowly and dress in something other than a Ronald McDonald costume. Wind might also put more bugs on the water or different ones than in calm conditions. And by the way, the only long season on most of these streams is winter. In other words, conditions relevant to fishing success can change quickly, so you had better be observant and capable of change.

The fish there are exceedingly shy too; they have to be to survive. These streams don't offer many places for fish to hide, either, by large water standards. The wise fisherman will hang back a bit, check out conditions, watch the stream and the stream banks, and really look closely for likely trout holding stations, best approach opportunities, insect activity, and so forth. Fish in these streams don't generally have a long growing season so they are quite opportunistic in their feeding habits. This simply means that if you do your part, they'll do theirs.

It's also fair to say that small streams offer a limited space to expand their resident trout population, thus the fish present (especially Brook Trout) can exceed the food supply and become stunted. Maybe you should keep a few for breakfast. It's also possible the deep pool you're looking at holds a really big fish that has learned to eat the little ones, thank you very much! One of us missed such a trout last September when he fished "a little Brookie stream" and didn't bother to carry a net. That fish was close to eighteen inches long and might still live in a pool no more than ten feet long by five feet wide and three feet deep! Hardly enough room to tire him out on the end of a light tippet and of course that was the problem. Luckily, we never have to stop learning, and someone certainly went to school with that fine trout! Oh yeah, how that exceptional trout probably got there will be revealed in a later chapter entitled "Where Are These Wonderful Streams?"

It's also true that small streams may be easily abused or "fished out." In other words, they generally will be in delicate balance. So when you find an obscure small stream, or a hidden section of a well known one, it deserves a great deal of thought, respect, and care. As do the fish in it. More on that subject later.

In the meantime start making some adjustments of your fishing thought processes to encompass the small stream environment. Maybe you could re-read this chapter to begin with.

"From April until September when the trout leaps, fish for him with a dubbed hook suitable to the month."
The Treatyse of Fysshynge with An Angle (1496)

The chapter title is, of course, an intuitively obvious statement. But most fishermen new to small streams seem to keep their fly everywhere BUT in the stream! It appears the natural thing for a small stream novice to do is to step briskly up the stream bank, stand up straight, let out some line and start false casting – again and again. This might be picturesque, and true to the movie *A River Runs Through It*, but it don't catch trout from small streams! The practice does tend to catch willow branches, high grass and the spruce tree across the stream, though, thus screwing up that carefully crafted image you'd like to project. And the fish will notice, too. Do fish laugh?

After some degree of study, we now estimate that extracting a fly from the brush, high grass, stream side rocks, etc., or tying on a new one takes at least as much time as five or six careful casts. And maybe more if your hands are cold or you see a really nice trout rising just ahead! Think about all that wasted time! This concept is really important because you could literally spend (waste?) most of your fishing time on a stream in the "penalty box," to borrow a term from hockey, just getting untangled or re-rigging. We don't know about you, but after we've walked a couple of hours (or more) up the mountain to get there, we want to fish the stream rather than the surrounding countryside. And the best streams usually do take awhile to get to. And it's always uphill going in or coming out. Or both. Not only is the time element worth considering but every time you have to extract a fly from the willows near the stream, you spook every trout in that section or pool. So you've wasted time AND scared the fish off! This simple insight is a lot more important than most fishermen think it is – evidently.

Let us count the ways an angler can get in the penalty box:

- Excessive or unnecessary false casting,
- inaccurate casting,
- inadequate room for the selected cast, especially its back cast,
- poor casting technique,
- setting the hook too enthusiastically, and
- wind.

As you see, most of the variables that cost you effective fishing time are controllable by the angler. Hello?

So how do you avoid wasting the stream? Generally the key for most of us is to keep a minimum amount of line in your cast. Use only what you need to avoid spooking the trout and figure ways to shorten that (such as shooting line, more stealth, etc.), if possible. Select the spot from which to cast as carefully as the point to which you wish to cast, that is, your target. Don't worry about whether or not you'll know if you are spooking the fish; the shallow water will usually allow you to see them scooting for cover if you get too close! Sometimes you'll just see their wake, or an unexplained silt cloud in the water, though. Or you don't raise a fish from that perfect spot. Even after several casts though you've made good presentations with a proven fly.

Short casts help you minimize the effects of brush, trees, and other obstacles near your back cast, improve casting accuracy, and reduce the impact of wind. Therefore your fly will be in the water more – where the trout can see it. Clearly it's also important to check where your back cast will go before you initiate your cast. And it's also easy to cast too far (remember, it's a small stream), thus hanging up on the opposite bank, so know how much line you need to place your fly where you want it.

False casting to dry your fly can lead to problems, too, if you don't stay tuned to your environment. In fact, you might be more apt to let your guard down while false casting than while really fishing. Nothing against false casting, of course, just keep in mind you have other options to dry your fly if needed. A truly dry fly is easier to see and is, most of the time, more effective than a drowned one.

A long cast feels (and looks) good if there is room for your back cast and if you can hit the stream on your forward cast, but can you manage your line once the fly and line are on the water? If you can't keep the fly drifting naturally you spook the fish just about as bad as if you were too close. There is a trade-off between staying out of the trout's sight with a long cast (with its associated difficulties in achieving a natural drift) and a short cast that puts you in the fish's view and thus spooks it.

Simple, huh? What follows in Chapter Six are some suggestions that can help you implement this obvious, but frequently ignored, key to success. In the meantime there are some additional basic ideas important to small stream fishing we wish to introduce.

"Here comes the trout that must be caught with tickling"
The Twelfth Night, Act II, Scene I
William Shakespeare

"The fish can see you" – a comment we've used more than once to remind frustrated friends new to small stream fishing that the fish can see them. And having done so, the trout have stopped feeding for awhile or scooted off to their hidey hole. The idea of stealth on the stream may be the second most important idea in the book. (Or maybe the first!) Remember, the stream is shallow and clear, the fish have natural enemies from above and so they have learned to be very cautious. Therefore, if they detect you, they are usually unavailable to catch. You've probably seen the generally accepted diagram of a fish's viewing area or limits. It looks like an inverted cone or funnel with a wider view as the fish approaches the surface of the water it's holding in. The experts tell us that "cone of vision" is fixed at ninety-seven degrees but effectively widens at the water's surface to near 160 degrees due to the refraction of light as it enters water from the atmosphere. So fish can see things in a large area, however light refraction also creates distortion at the edge of the cone. And they have the ability to simultaneously focus on objects both near and far! If you wish to remain out of their clear view, stay low – really low. Sometimes even prone, surely on your knees, and crouched over even when you are ten or fifteen yards (not feet) away from the stream. Move slowly as well, since even with substantial distortion, rapid movement can easily be detected by the fish. Or maybe you can use those pesky willows as cover to approach your casting position, or possibly a large rock will do. They can see better upstream than downstream, over their back. So, all else being equal, you can get closer with an upstream approach than with a downstream approach. In fact, the area "over their shoulder" is, as far as anglers are concerned, the trout's only blind spot.

Trout can also see colors and, obviously, patterns. The clothing you wear can thus be important as can bright, shiny things hanging off your fishing vest. We think it's best to wear subdued colors that blend into the stream's background, and keep the shiny accessories in your pockets. Camouflage clothing is even worth considering except during hunting season. As mentioned above, move slowly; rapid movement always catches the attention of wildlife, and fish are no exception. So jerking on your line when your fly is caught in an overhanging willow branch will scare 'em, too. See how this stuff goes together? If you hang up anywhere near the trout you're trying to catch, you're probably done for; finished; you've spooked the trout. Rats! (Or stronger).

Always look for the opportunity to sneak up on 'em; you'll find this is fun just by itself. It appeals to the kid in us all. In fact, you must sneak up on 'em. And, if you are really stealthy, you'll catch more and larger trout. We should point out that the reverse of this principle is also true. Stealthy fishing embodies a test; will you pass?

Oh, did we mention that the fish can hear you, too? Well they can, and very well indeed. They have an inner ear but no external nor middle ear. The latter are not necessary because water conducts sound better than air and the density of water is near that of the trout's body, so sound is readily conducted to the inner ear. In addition, trout can pick up vibrations, changes in pressure, and chemicals (scents) in the water with organs along their lateral line. Vibrations travel especially well in water and through marshy bank structure. The practical implications to us fishermen are to avoid wading, if possible, and then only with great care. And stop stomping around on the banks! Seeing is believing, so feel free to run a couple of experiments to test the need for stealth near streams. In fact we encourage you to do so as this will do much to enhance our credibility. But first you must approach the stream with enough care to see that the fish will flee when you do something to disturb the water! If you run up there stomping around and talking rapidly with your hands, they will have disappeared before you arrived. Look for silt clouds and wakes in the quiet water to confirm their former locations.

We don't know if voicing one's frustration about hanging up once again in the willows will scare trout; you might get away with that if you're not too loud. And if you can success-fully emulate the sounds and rhythm of a passing deer or other non-threatening wildlife maybe you don't even have to worry about tromping around in the stream or on its banks. Might be worth a try if you are naturally clumsy.

How about this scent thing? Some of our experience suggests trout are put off by insect repellent odors on flies handled after applying the stuff to exposed parts of our bodies. You may also be aware of special preparations designed to enhance warm water fishermen's success. We are not snobs and have no problem with such an approach for catfish and bass; in fact we've all caught more than a few bass and catfish, even some with stink bait! We just don't think these preparations fit well into respectable fly fishing for trout. We sure don't claim to be experts on this one, but keeping your hands clean when handling flies and such seems to be in order. (We don't have much data on the effects of more pleasant odors such as after shave, perfume and bourbon but, for goodness sakes, we're talking about fishing here, not a dinner party.) However some of these scents might attract bears to your location. Finally, remember the observation from Chapter Two about events in and around small streams being relatively more significant than the same event in large waters? Well?

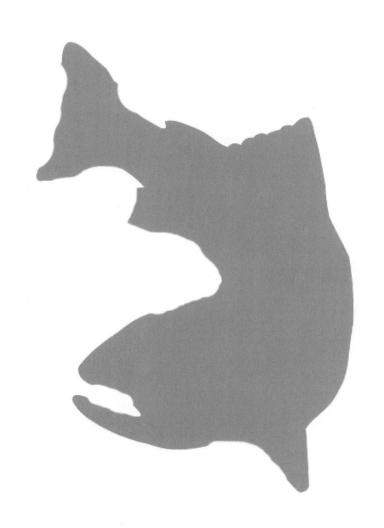

Chapter Five
Where's the Trout?

"Yes; there is nothing pays better with good fish than a little careful preliminary study of their territory."
Francis Francis, *A Book on Angling* (1867)

The trout have the home field advantage. "Home field advantage;" think about the implications of that statement. The trout lives in the stream; you just visit it. They have the home field advantage. They choose when to feed and what to eat. They are where they want to be; all the time (until you catch 'em). They know where to go to avoid predators or threats (you). We don't suggest that trout have cognitive abilities; however, their inbred instincts for survival and procreation evidently lead them to make "choices" or form successful habits. They are unlikely to change these habits just because you show up on the stream. Even if you're famous. Or the best fisherman in your town. Or the best dressed. In other words, you must adapt to their habits with your fishing techniques; they won't change to meet your previously established style or the techniques you recently used successfully on the San Juan River. Nor have they heard the latest stories about your fishing expertise. In other words, they have the home field advantage and you can't change that. You must adapt to it. Relax, be modest. The fish is in charge here.

It's not that they don't have any respect for you; it's just that they don't care. They are mostly focused on consuming more calories than they expend, while avoiding predators. Occasionally they breed. It's a good idea to remember these obvious little facts (or check around for evidence of worm fishermen) when you're not catching fish on an otherwise perfect stream. You might as well be a good student, because you're not going to teach the fish anything except how to be more wary. Certainly, they will not adapt their habits to your style.

This fact leads to a mindset and is the very reason why the best anglers enjoy fly fishing. It's the direct opposite of today's all-too-frequent philosophy of "It's All About Me!" The natural challenge in an environment other than one made by man builds character rather than ego.

So how do we then level the playing field? Well, the trout's natural habits hold the answer. We will take their "home field advantage" and use elements of it as indicators of the places where trout will most likely lie. Once we know that, we can then develop strategies to catch trout consistently!

To answer the key question of fish location we suggest you do the obvious, and easiest, thing first; study the stream carefully. Look for disturbances made by feeding fish on the water's surface and look into the water for trout shapes and shadows. Sometimes you can see the trout you wish to catch. You should try to. If you can frequently see the fish or their rise forms from a good casting position, while it is unaware or unconcerned with your presence, you are practicing an effective stealthy approach. Congratulations!

Sometimes, however, you need to "fish the water" using good judgment and the suggestions in this book as your guide to fish location. In a small stream it's not unusual to have only one good opportunity to catch a specific trout, especially the best one in the pool. Sometimes an unsuccessful cast or presentation will spook all the fish in your selected section of the stream. Thus knowing where to place your fly is important to your success. Most of the time we can count on trout being in one of two places; a feeding lie or a hiding lie. Occasionally they are in transit. As in larger water, feeding lies occur at current seams, near rocks or other obstructions in the stream, under foam lines, in riffles, etc. Small streams just offer smaller, harder to see feeding and hiding lies. Some of these can really surprise you. When you (inevitably) spook a nice trout from that place you didn't see, take time to inspect the area. Look at it from where you were just before the trout zipped away. Try to find the specific initial location of the trout. Maybe this observation will help you see a similar lie next time. Also, try to see where that trout fled to; you might wish to fish it (or a similar lie) when the trout is not so concerned about its safety. If you end the day on a good small stream without spooking a single trout, you are either (a) on a picnic, (b) oblivious, or (c) really an excellent fisherman! Most of us tend to get in a hurry to approach that obvious lie up ahead and miss the fish under our feet. Probing any possible holding place for feeding or hiding trout is part of the fun. Don't miss it.

Many small streams are scoured by spring run-off and thus offer limited (and also harder to see) hiding places for trout. They are then forced to become adept at concealment in unexpected places; unexpected to anglers, that is. Many small streams sport excellent undercut banks; custom made to hold nice trout. We've seen meadow streams with only about two feet of visible water surface, but at least another foot or so of undercut on each bank. Can you get your fly in there; maybe even with no drag? Don't overlook the shady places under willows or tree overhangs or, obviously, deeper water either. The ideal location for a trout, and thus the place holding the largest fish around, is a combo location offering both feeding opportunity and concealment. Those undercut banks qualify, as do lots of locations shielded by low vegetation overhangs or deep shadows. If it looks hard to get a fly under there, you've probably got a really good spot! Even if someone's been on this section of the stream before you, they likely couldn't put an effectively drifted fly just there. Maybe that fish has never even seen an artificial fly! Wow! Think of the possibilities!

We offered our opinion of what constitutes the ideal location for a trout. What do you think is next best? Would it be a location that offers feeding opportunities with concealment very near? Or concealment with feeding opportunity very near? And what's next best? Maybe more distance between the two defines the third best lie? And so on. So the best trout occupies the most ideal location in the pool, the next most competitive fish the next best lie, and the hierarchy of several trout in a pool is thereby established. They do it naturally and you can think it through. If you wish.

Chapter Six
Casting Effectively

"It is not easy to tell one how to cast.
The art must be acquired by practice."
Charles Orvis (1883)

In this chapter we discuss the wisdom of effective casting, but will not teach you how to cast. See the quote above. On the other hand, you need some idea of how a few specific casts can be executed and how they might be useful to the small stream angler. But it's difficult to teach casting techniques just by the written word; practice and example are needed; Mr. Orvis knew his business. There are a number of well written and illustrated books entirely about fly casting and these can be very helpful. Another approach to learning fly casting is via commercial video or search the internet; you'll find extensive resources in the form of YouTube videos. Competent personal instruction will accelerate the learning process and is available from professional instructors, local fly fishing clubs and sometimes an expert neighbor or fishing guide.

In our view the topic of "casting effectively" has two essential dimensions: the best cast for the situation and the accuracy of that cast. You can leave your double haul at home; the correct cast on small streams will emphasize finesse rather than distance. It's easy to spook these trout, so we want to use just enough line, softly laid on the water, to drift a fly, without drag, right by the fish you want to strike. Remember, you might not be able to see the fish but you can easily imagine where it is and anyway you should fish the same way for the fish you can't see as one you can. Easy, Huh? You already know the basics, or perhaps this is a good time to contact someone adept at teaching fly casting.

In addition to standard overhead and side casts, several special casts can be helpful. The Slingshot cast is downright surgical when executed properly, albeit only for close work. Such as under those low overhangs we mentioned earlier. A pile cast can be just right for the occasional drift downstream into an otherwise unreachable hole. Or a curve cast because you'll spook the fish if you even begin to ease around that bend or rock. Roll casts and the Steeple cast serve well in situations with limited back cast space. The more of these specialty casts you have in your skill set, the better you'll be able to take advantage of the opportunities offered by crafty fish in small streams. If you are fishing on Western small streams you are wise to learn how to cast into the wind and across the wind and with the wind because the wind will often impact your cast, especially in those wonderful open meadows with the stream meandering through.

Still, even with the correct cast selection, you have to put the fly where the fish is, or very close. These trout seldom want to move very far to have a meal, so they don't. A major reason which bears repeating because it's so important to your fishing strategy. To the trout it's a matter of survival; they must use less energy in capturing a meal than they gain by eating the meal. They are also more exposed to their predators when rising to a bug. That's gotta make them nervous.

A second reason the angler must place their fly close applies mostly to dry fly fishing. When a fish is holding close to the water's surface its "window" or viewing area at the surface is small. Your fly simply might not be noticed by these trout.

All of us suffer poor casts from time to time however, and we think one should always fish out a poor cast. If your cast goes astray, for whatever reason, but your fly lands in or on the water, fish it as if it was exactly what you intended to do. That is, "fish it out." Why? Two good reasons. One; because we all make enough fishing mistakes anyway, so why draw attention to them. Never can tell who might be watching. Second, and more importantly, it's possible our mistakes will cancel each other out and luck will kick in! Maybe you didn't see "**that**" fish! At worst, fishing the cast out will help prevent spooking the fish you did see. At best you'll catch a fish and at worst you'll have another chance. Win, Win. It's all about improving your chances of catching a fish.

Accurate casting also helps keep you out of the brush, streamside grass, etc., and there's nothing more frustrating than having to spook a nice trout just because you hung your fly or line on something. Consider again the benefits of accurate casts; putting the fly near the fish increases your chance of a take and those same good casts keep you out of trouble, giving you maximum presentation time to the object of your effort. Now, think about that still again from time to time.

It has been said that "to fly fish is to cast." And it's true, but what "they" didn't say was that the angler did not have to be an expert caster to fish successfully. To be sure, and as stated previously, the better one casts, the more successful a fisherman he or she will be. This is true simply because you scare fewer fish and can put your fly in the right place to solicit a strike when you can cast well. Thus there are fine rewards for learning to cast effectively. It's true on any water but we think especially so on small streams. With that in mind here are some "specialty" casts we think you'll want to learn in your journey to becoming a master small stream angler.

The Sling Shot or Bow & Arrow Cast

The Sling Shot or Bow and Arrow cast is a most useful cast on small streams. As mentioned previously, it has a limited range, but a good stealthy approach can go far to mitigate this limitation. This casting technique excels in situations where no room exists for a back cast or the target water is guarded by dense or overhanging brush, limbs and such. It is also a very accurate cast, so, with practice, its use will allow very precise placement of your fly.

The cast is executed by first pulling out from your rod's tip a length of line and leader, with the fly attached, equal to the rod's length plus a foot or so extra. A short leader with a little fly line extending from the tip top will be an advantage with this cast. Keep in mind that trout resident in the areas requiring a sling shot cast are not as likely to be leader shy as those in an open run. Secure your fly line against the rod grip with your right forefinger, holding the rod grip with your right thumb on top. Carefully grasp the fly between your left thumb and forefinger. Point the rod tip at your target with your right arm fully extended, then pull back, putting tension on the line and a bow into the tip of the fly rod. Now, still another reason for fishing barbless becomes obvious! Do not allow the line to slip through your right hand grip while you apply line tension with your left hand. Now pull back with your left hand as if drawing a bow and arrow, but back as far as your reach allows. Be aware of where the fly is relative to your ear lest you discover another reason to fish barbless! Keeping the immediately preceding statement in mind, release the fly from your left thumb and forefinger while keeping your right arm and your rod fully extended. The fly will be propelled forward along a path defined by the rod when fully straightened, that is, where you pointed it in the first place. With practice, you can even shoot a few inches more line with this cast, although your timing on releasing line at the rod grip will be important to success. Allowing your right wrist to break a little as you put tension in the line, then straightening it after fly release, as the rod load is released, can also help improve line speed and distance. Using this basic form, the angler can vary the angle of rod bend to achieve a vertical or horizontal cast or anything in between. To lay out a low cast, say under a low-hanging branch, just kneel, keep the rod low and the bow horizontal. The absence of a back cast of any kind will open up casting opportunities you probably have not considered previously. The brush-choked stream now becomes a possible and fine new opportunity for excellent fishing. The wise and elusive big old trout just became easier to fool!

A bonus with this cast is that it is easily and quickly learned, so beginners and kids can accelerate their success on stream. In our opinion, anything that softens a child's fly fishing learning curve is a good investment for an adult.

The Roll Cast

Only slightly more difficult than the Slingshot Cast is the Roll Cast. This one is as easy as one, two, three – literally. But you must start with some line on the water. Step one is to slowly but steadily lift your rod tip against the drag imposed by the water's surface on your line. When the rod tip is slightly behind your head, say one o'clock, pause a moment. Step two: bring the rod tip forward briskly then abruptly stop the forward cast at, say eleven o'clock. Step three is to watch your fly line roll out in front of you and, as it straightens, lower your rod tip to complete the cast. With practice one can shoot considerable amount of line but even a novice can cast fifteen or twenty feet of fly line plus leader. This one works better with weight forward lines. It has the great advantage of not requiring back cast room so those situations of brush at your back are not nearly so intimidating.

The Steeple Cast

This is one of those casting techniques that is not based on finesse! You use it in areas where fly presentation is not important, you just need to get the fly into position to drift through the identified feeding lane. This cast is generally used on turbulent streams with lots of structure along the banks, but not much trouble over head. Grasp the rod for a traditional cast with your thumb on top of the rod; it will be your aiming device. Feed line out letting the current carry the fly and line down stream (but you're going to cast upstream). When you have enough line out to reach the target area, bring the rod up so that it is pointing straight up in the air like the steeple on a church. Stop your motion, make sure you have enough line out to allow at least the fly and leader to remain on the surface of the water. The leader and fly in the flowing water will cause the rod to be loaded when starting the following casting motion. Now with a very aggressive arm movement, move the arm and rod from pointing straight up to pointing straight at your target area. Your target area should be upstream from the area you want the fly to drift through so that the current will deliver the fly to the feeding fish. Try to position yourself so that fly line and the feeding lane form about a sixty degree angle when it hits the water, as this will reduce the probability of spooking the fish when the fly line hits the water and will help keep the moving rod out of the fish's vision.

This is a hard cast to practice without a pool of water or, even better, a moving stream, but it is a very simple cast to master.

The Pile Cast

The pile cast and its relatives are useful when the angler is dealing with complex currents such as those found near oxbow bends and in shallow water with large rocks which shift the water around. They are also very useful in downstream situations where the stream flows under low-hanging limbs, willows, and such. In other words, the pile cast earns its keep in situations where extra slack in the fly line is needed to allow a drift-free presentation of the fly. And it's easy to learn. Execute an overhead cast, but stop your rod sharply at about eleven o'clock. You want to stop the rod firmly enough to cause the fly line to rebound somewhat as it is straightening out before you. This puts waves into the line. Now lower the rod more slowly to preserve those waves onto the water's surface. Another variation, sometimes called the "Serpentine Cast" has the angler stop his rod high in the forward cast, then wiggle the rod tip horizontally to create the waves in the fly line. We suggest you try both techniques and select the one that works best for you; they both accomplish the same objective, that is, putting a controlled amount of slack in the line before it hits the water. Accuracy with this type cast has more to do with placing the fly in the correct current (feeding lane) than placing the fly near the fish, but it is effective because it can deliver the fly in a very natural way to the fish. Re-read that last sentence because this could be the cast to pull the big one out from under the overhang or cut bank! You know, the wise old fish that has learned to be very leader shy and has grown fat on the knowledge!

The Curve Cast

How many times have you had this situation come up: you are working your way up a stream only to have a willow hanging out over the water and just upstream from the willow there is a fine fish feeding on the surface? What can you do? Well, move to the other side of the stream. This might work, but you stand a good chance of putting the fish down (that is, scaring it so that it stops feeding or it flees to a safer location) as you lose your cover or stumble on a slick rock. You could get your buddy's attention;

he is already on the other side working his way up to you. By the way, did I mention this is a nineteen inch native Rio Grande Cutthroat! Do you really want to chance spooking her? Or, dare we say it; share? There's another way out of this potentially sticky moral dilemma.

Let's throw a curve just like a pitcher does when he wants to brush back the batter and drop it in for a strike. This cast makes use of the traditional cast, with one added motion. You know, pick the rod up, lifting the fly off the water, send it into your back cast, stopping the rod at 1:00, let the rod load, then come forward to about 12:00; at this point drive your arm straight forward, still in the 12:00 position, and with your arm extended, break your wrist forward so that rod is now at 10:00. This is where the part that makes the fly curve around the willow comes in.

Let's set the scene; you are on the left hand side of the stream as you look upstream and the willow upstream is also on the left side. So you want the fly to go upstream, pass the willow then curve to the left and softly land on the upstream side of the willow. Now back to the cast: you have just snapped your wrist forward, the fly has gone screaming by your ear, and is passing the willow as well as starting to reach its full forward motion. Now move the rod tip up and to the right, more right than up. Let's say the rod tip is drawing a line in the sky, moving to the right less than forty-five degrees up from the horizon. The dynamics of all this gyration causes the fly to move to the left and settle in behind the willow; the fish looks up, and the fly lands in his feeding lane. You have the fish and your buddy wants you to teach him the trick cast you just pulled off! Instead of fussing at you for not having given him a chance at that trophy trout, you have just caught a nice fish and preserved a relationship!

Fly Casting in Windy Conditions

Especially on Western small streams, wind is either present or soon will be. So learning to successfully place your fly on the water in the wind is a real gateway to predictable fishing success. We focus here on casting into or with the wind as we're pretty sure you'll know how to adjust your cast when the wind is crossways. If not, the wind will tell you how to adjust your next cast. Just watch where your fly went versus where you wanted it to go and make the necessary adjustments, right? Of course, it's also wise to keep the fly downwind of you as you cast. Otherwise you might receive an unplanned piercing through your ear, nose, or other body part. Although planned piercings seem to be popular nowadays.

In really windy conditions the sling shot cast and a stealthy approach can keep you fishing instead of just trying to get a cast out. Its secret of success is simply having little line out (to be impacted by the wind) and no back cast. The range of a sling shot cast is limited but its success characteristics are worth thinking about as you consider how to get your fly on the water near a trout with the wind giving you fits. This is especially appropriate when the conditions of brush near the stream and wind present themselves together.

A major consideration when casting in windy conditions is to keep your cast line in places where the wind is least severe; this generally means low to the ground. Golfers know what we mean. But it can also mean shielding your cast from the worst of the wind using whatever natural wind breaks offered by your environment; trees, brush and canyons. However, it's our general experience that canyons channel wind right along the stream so they most often offer more problems than solutions. Nonetheless, the idea is to think about how you're going to deal with wind rather than just going back to camp, moaning and complaining. (It's an attitude thing.) Consider wind just another challenge and be pleased you can still fish when others might give it up. With that in mind here are some additional suggestions to help you thwart that pesky wind. Thwart is such a good word! Say it out loud -- "Thwart the wind!" Say it again! You're already half way there! But your partner might have a weird expression just now.

You've already read about the first best rule; keep your line low. The second best rule for windy conditions is keep your line short. The more time the wind has to act on your cast the worse you'll like the result. We wish there was a third best rule, then we'd have a trifecta; but keeping the fly downwind in cross wind casts is a good candidate.

Although it's debatable whether casting into the wind or with the wind at your back is worse, we most often hear about the difficulty in casting into the wind, so we'll start with that condition. Remember earlier we suggested that the small stream angler should "leave his double haul at home"? Well here's the exception that proves the rule. While the double or single haul are casts normally used by fly fishermen to cast a long line, here we use a double haul (or a single haul on the forward cast) to get some speed into the line. Not for distance, but for penetration into the wind. The objective here is not to shoot line, but to get through that wind. You needn't have a lot of line out for a haul to work for you, even though we usually think of a haul associated with long casts. The haul does two things that are good for your cast into the wind: it makes a smaller loop and it speeds up the whole cast. Not shooting line with the haul actually makes it easier to use. Keep your practice simple. Keep your cast brisk; no slop allowed. Use a swift tug, starting with your line hand at the stripper, when you pick up at the beginning of your cast. Let this hand drift back up to the stripper as the line stretches out behind you. Give the line that same smart tug as you start your forward cast and the line will express right through the wind as you complete the cast.

A couple of techniques can be useful when casting with the wind at your back. One is the good ol' roll cast. Wind at your back will help carry line out front but you have a back cast into the wind to worry about. The roll cast is executed by first taking up any slack from your line on the water then slowly raise the rod tip up allowing the rod to load against the surface tension of the water. When the tip is at about one o'clock or slightly less, pause very briefly then make a brisk forward stroke with the rod stopping firmly at about ten o'clock. The fly line will form a loop which will roll out and straighten as it runs out of line.

Another way to use the wind to your advantage is to change the plane of your cast. Keep your back cast short and let it almost fall to the surface behind you. Then cast forward but aim up, perhaps as much as forty-five degrees and stop your forward cast early, say at one o'clock. The wind will pick up your line and move it down wind, that is, in front of you. Have some line ready to feed out (shoot) as the wind does your work for you. Clearly this cast works best when you don't have a bunch of stuff like tall grass or willows behind you. But the stronger the wind is, the better this cast will work!

Finally, the most obvious tactic for windy conditions; and this one takes little description. Simply change the plane of your normal overhead cast to bring it more horizontal. Some refer to this as a "side arm cast." Regardless of the name, it works by keeping the line in the softer wind near the ground or water surface. As always, practice is a key to accuracy, and thus effectiveness, and the side arm cast is no exception. Your loop will be straightening out in a plane ninety degrees to your normal aiming plane so proper execution, allowing it to fully straighten just above the water's surface will be even more important than in the overhead cast. And even low to the surface the wind is still present, just not so bad as higher up.

A Final Bonus From Casting Practice

Again, we suggest plenty of practice on your lawn, or at a local park. That means before you arrive in the area near where you'll fish; indeed, this casting preparation may be the most important thing you can do off stream to be successful on stream! Except buying a fine, custom bamboo fly rod. Your lawn practice target should be no more than about ten or twelve inches in diameter and you should be able to put your fly on the target under the ideal conditions of lawn casting seven or eight times out of ten at ten, twenty and thirty feet. The practice is even more useful if you conduct it occasionally in the wind and/or with bushes back of you.

As a bonus, casting practice is a lot like walking a nice dog; it interests lots of folks so your social interactions might broaden quite a bit. You can be selective by looking like you're having fun (attract) or looking very serious in your efforts (discourage). We think you are smart enough to figure this one out. Now you have two goals; both fun.

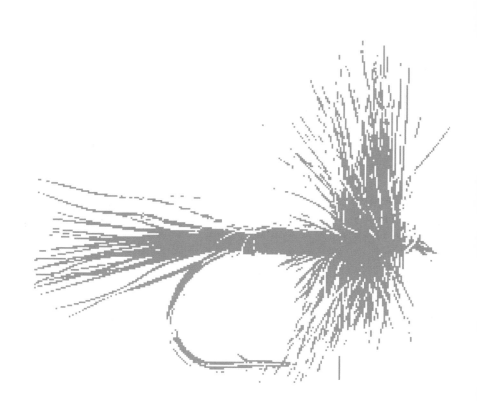

Chapter Seven
Wakes, Slack and Natural Bugs

"No one can doubt the existence of reason in lower animals who has once seen an old educated trout carefully examine the angler's floating fly, follow it down a yard or two scrutinizing it. See! He scornfully wags his tail, he has recognized the deception, he returns to his former station and absolutely refuses now to take the slightest notice of anything in the fur and feather line."

**J. C. Mottram, Fly-fishing: Some New Arts and Mysteries
(1915)**

By their nature, trout will take advantage of every error you make while fishing (as well as some errors you make while not fishing). Also by nature, fish, especially those in small streams, must ever be on the watch for food and will refuse it only when the danger of going after it is larger, or its energy value less, than the reward of nutrition. So that means in our sport of angling the fish will generally do its part. Perhaps if you're not catching fish it's probably your fault. That's tough for most of us to admit, but it's true. When you pause to realize that is the situation, then you can address your opportunities for improvement.

And for goodness sake, don't put it off. Delaying action by "just a few more casts" or "I'll just try the next hole" may sum up as a "slow day"!

All we are trying to do when fishing small streams is to fool the fish into reacting to our fly in the same way it reacts to natural food. (In other words this book, like all of them on fly fishing, could be just one sentence written on a slip of paper – but we couldn't charge much for it and it wouldn't include suggested techniques for success, anyway.) We fool the fish by introducing flies that imitate natural bugs and other trout food in appearance and in behavior into or on the water, without disturbing the fish. Once fooled into striking our fly, we then want to connect the fish to our line by way of a hook, preferably in the trout's mouth. One philosophy of fishing is to eliminate any activity on our part not consistent with those objectives. With that philosophy in mind, it's easy to understand why a fly that is dragging or producing even the smallest of wakes is not good form (except in very unusual and special circumstances such as imitating a "fluttering caddis"). Drag, or a wake, associated with most fly presentations tells all the local trout "I'm a fake!" So you are well advised to keep a bit of slack in your tippet.

But not too much! Too much slack in your line, leader, and tippet will prevent you from setting the hook on a timely basis. In other words, you'll "miss him." This is especially a problem when fishing upstream in rapidly moving water – which is most of the time on small streams. "How ya doin'? Oh, I've caught one and missed about ten."

Unfortunately, it is hard to learn the correct amount of slack by fishing the lawn or local park. You have to learn this one on the stream. The good news is that most every strike is a learning opportunity with a test already in place. (Still another pithy

36

and important sentence! Please re-read it for emphasis.) The basic starting point solution is pretty straightforward.

Just keep in mind that most folks allow way too much slack in their line when they are fishing upstream and too little when fishing across or downstream. It might be safe to say something more comprehensive than "most." Try "all" fishermen new to small streams. So it will be OK for you to strip in line aggressively when you are fishing upstream and allow an "S" or two in your line when fishing down or across stream. You'll have the opportunity to refine this approach as the tests occur. Be different. Catch a fish.

Speaking of slack; what do you do with all that line that accumulates around you feet when you strip it in without winding it on your reel? It's your choice, but that line can lose you a fish if it gets tangled up in your feet, rocks, brush in the stream, or whatever. Maybe you could consider storing it where it should be stored: on your reel! Those things are pretty but they have a purpose, too.

A good bass fisherman will tell you that you should wait until you can feel the fish on your line before you set the hook.

And that's good advice for bass fishing with a plastic worm in still water. But not for trout fishing in high mountain streams. It seems the higher elevation trout, especially cuttbows and native cutthroats, don't take much time over a meal. They are fast and efficient! Our observation is consistent with the conditions of survival in high mountain streams. The seasons for eating, growing, and procreating are short, so the successful trout will be looking for its next meal as it swallows the present one. If you can't keep up with your fly (that means see your dry fly, or indicator when you're nymphing) or feel your nymph 'ticking' along the stream bottom, you are going to miss some nice trout. The trout will eject it before you know you've had a strike. Now, we'll admit, sometimes knowing where your fly should be is the best you can do, especially with small flies. Well, that will have to do; but you'd best know at least as much as that! When you've lost contact with your fly, even if a trout takes it with an obvious splash, the chances are good you'll be too late with your set. Reaction time, you see; and the fish is faster than you. Plus she started before you did. By the time her take gives you a hint as to where the fly is and you set the hook, she's already decided it wasn't good to eat. And spit it out.

Now we all know it takes the fish a finite amount of time to take in the fly, decide it's not good to eat, and eject it. To be consistently effective in setting the hook, sometimes it's almost like the angler must meet the striking fish halfway. If you're in visual contact with your fly, either directly or by watching the end of your fly line or some other type indicator, you can see the take begin and can initiate the set before the fish has time to eject the fly. Encouragingly, this can work even if you've lost contact with the fly! Sounds tough? With some practice and education of your eye, it's really not. Many times the feeding trout will give you a hint that it has eaten your fly. Here are some examples of the beginning of a take, or strike. You see a flash of white near where your nymph should be. (It's the fish opening its mouth to suck in your fly) Your fly line or other indicator pauses or moves in a way not indicated by the current. (The trout just inhaled your fly, maybe even started to run off with it.) You see the water swell or move, other than the current, near your dry fly. (It's the trout moving to your fly.) There was a flash or you think you saw some other type of movement near your fly. (Duh.) Oops, sorry 'bout that. Clearly, the more experienced fishermen will set the hook on these indicators and other ones that careful observation will reveal to you. (Read closely now, the next sentence is real important.) Yeah, you might miss a few trout by being too quick, but the chances that the trout will take a second attempt are much better with a premature set than when it has spit out your fly on a slow set. The above statement makes sense; in the first case the fish still thinks your fly is food, maybe even more so, because it just moved. In the second case the fish already decided your fly was not food, then ejected it. Try the experiment; you'll see. And when you get it right, it really feels good!

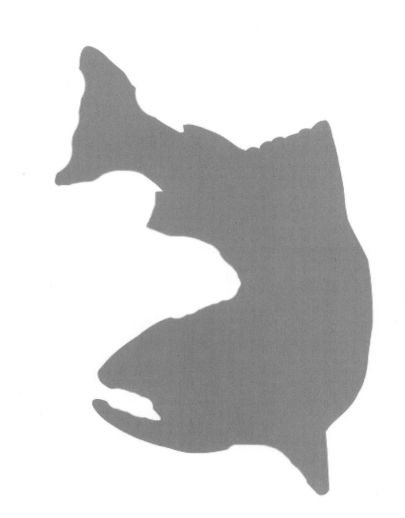

Chapter Eight
Situations and Strategies

"Listen to the sound of the river and you will get a trout"
Irish proverb

Every type of water; be it pond, lake, river or small stream has its own set of unique fishing situations. Understanding the characteristics or key elements of these situations is an essential step to developing the fishing strategy most likely to yield your desired result.

In Chapter Two we introduced some thought-provoking (we hope) comments about how small streams are different from other fishing venues. And in Chapter Five we discussed some general ideas about small stream trout habits and habitats. Here we will probe specific fishing situations common on small streams and offer comments on useful strategies for success when you encounter these situations.

At the risk of re-stating the obvious, all these situations are set up by the environment, which includes the fish, so studying that environment and the implications it has on our quarry is a most important consideration for the angler. Our intent is not so much to offer a rigid recipe for success as it is to introduce some options intended to stimulate your assessment of your specific fishing situation and your resulting strategy. This approach is consistent with our opinion that optimal enjoyment of fishing is more aligned with catching specific, targeted trout by successfully emulating nature than by having a "fifty-trout or one hundred-trout day." Otherwise the sub-title of our book would be something like *SUGGESTIONS FOR SUCCESSFUL USE OF BIG NETS ON SMALL STREAMS.* On the other hand, stringing together a long sequence of successful strategies can result in some pretty impressive catch numbers. If you count daily totals. We generally don't. The number of fish you caught in a given day doesn't matter, right? Right?

Pools are common in any good trout stream, so let's start there. There are two obvious first questions (and resulting strategies) pertaining to any pool; what size is the best fish in the pool and how many fish are there in the pool? If the pool in question is small the answer to both questions might be obtained by catching only one fish from it. If you think the pool is large enough to support more than one fish then you've got a dilemma; should you go for the best fish in the pool or see how many you can catch from the pool. The strategy probably isn't the same for both questions. For the "best fish" you will need to determine where the safest, most energy-productive, spot is. 'Cause that's where the dominate fish in that pool is and that fish is almost sure to be the best (biggest) fish in the pool, especially if the pool has not been seriously disrupted in the recent past. Do not underestimate what it took for that fish to be in that lie. It got there because it has been more successful at surviving and growing than its peers, which means it is bigger, more agile and has better instincts (i.e., "smarter") than its peers. It won't be the easiest fish in the pond to catch; probably the most difficult. Which is why you're going

to try to catch it, right? So look for the best lie available in the pool. Remember Chapter Seven? How many chances do you have to place your carefully selected fly to drift naturally over or through that lie without disturbing it? Likely a number close to one. Partially because that best fish will not tolerate much of an error before it quits feeding or spooks, and partially because some other fish in the pool were likely spooked by your line on your first or second cast. They, of course, spooked the target trout.

How about if you're curious about the number of fish in the pool and you wish to see how many you can catch? Then the strategy might be to progressively catch fish from the bottom of the pool up to the top, quickly removing each (and releasing them downstream) before they frighten others nearby. You can easily see why careful study of the pool and likely lies can be of great assistance in selecting and sequencing casting targets to execute this strategy.

Visible trout in a pool can really be fun, and challenging as well. It's probably safe to assume the visible fish is feeding, unless it saw you before you saw it. (Think about it.) So, when you can see your target fish and it is still feeding, the strategy is simply to place your correctly chosen fly upstream of the trout in its feeding lane without drift and without spooking the fish. This is easier said than done, due to the variables involved. You can do it, though. The variables include, but are not limited to, fly choice, water depth and speed, and current variations due to stream topography.

Riffles are common in small streams and they also offer great sport and education to the astute angler. You are likely to see them either above or below a pool, or both. Sometimes one can

see trout in riffles, sometimes not; with correspondingly different strategies. When fish cannot be seen, it's frequently productive to work stream bottom structure as indicated by the water's surface; around larger rocks, at drop offs into deeper water, slightly deeper water (as indicated by a change in apparent water color), bubble lines, and the like. Fishing for visible fish in riffles is similar to fishing for them in pools, except they are frequently more difficult to see even though the water is shallower. So the trick here is to train your eye to see them, their shadow, movement, or other indicators (refer back to Chapter Five).

Bends and Oxbows frequently offer the best fishing to be had in small streams. These changes in the course of the stream result in strongly varied structure and water conditions in a short distance. With a flick of their tail trout can move from feeding stations in riffles, runs, and pools to the near absolute security of deeply undercut banks. Clearly this circumstance is very attractive to trout so bends and oxbows frequently hold the

best fish in the stream. Bends and oxbows have basically the same configuration; a low bank with relatively shallow water on the inside of the stream curve and a high bank with deeper water on the outside of the curve. The oxbow is simply a concentrated bend, so our comments about bends apply equally to them. Both are frequently characterized by a riffle upstream of the bend and one downstream of the bend. These riffles should be fished according to the suggestions above. The low bank will frequently consist of a gravel bar with a gradual slope into the depth of the stream. Quiet water prevails near this gravel bar and often it forms a mild whirlpool nearby. This whirlpool will concentrate food and thus hold fish but is difficult to fish due to its circular current and the resulting varied directions of fish orientation. Carefully watch the whirlpool surface and bottom, if possible, for feeding fish; such observation will guide you in selecting a stealthy location from which to cast, as well as the best fly placement. Without such guidance, cast willy-nilly into the whirlpool and hope that random events will result in a strike. There, that felt good, didn't it? What a relief from all this disciplined fishing! But back to business. Unless in very rocky terrain, the high bank will concentrate the fastest current in the bend and will be undercut. This is a great place for trout and your best fly placement is close to the bank starting just above the transition from riffle to deeper water as the bend begins. Trout will also concentrate just below and along the area where the riffle drops into deeper water, even somewhat removed from the "hot spot" described above.

Look on the next page. See the spot where the current is pushed out into the stream by the projecting left bank? There's a nice trout in the quiet water just behind the slightly darker flaring current.

Undercut banks, whether they be in bends as mentioned above or along grassy banks next to pools, runs, or riffles, are some of the most likely places to find trophy trout in small streams. They are worth careful study and thorough attention with your best fishing skills. Obviously undercut banks

offer a trout wonderful concealment and protection from most predators; natural ones as well as us fly fishermen. They also frequently have associated with them water currents which concentrate the fish's natural food into feeding lanes. These feeding lanes are often indicated on the water's surface by a bubble line. Sometimes they are more subtle and located under the water's surface. But they must be (or must have been) there; how else would an undercut be formed. Undercuts in pools are most likely to have light or even non-existent currents associated with them; the undercuts having been formed when the water levels and flows were higher. So, undercuts in pools may offer trout mostly protection and undercuts in bends, riffles, and runs can offer both protection and high profit food delivery. Does it then surprise you that trout in these preferred holding lies can get large, fat, and perhaps lazy? Can you see where this is going? Right! These fish are sometimes difficult to invite out to play. They can simply be picky and wait for the next food morsel to drift by. Here's where your hard-won casting, observation skills and the lessons of the early chapters of this book can really pay off. Probably the most technically challenging of the undercut situations is the one with a smooth run associated with it. In this situation the trout is well hidden and has the most undistorted view of potential predators above the water's surface. So, indeed, it might amount to the final exam for the student of small stream fishing. Stealth, fly selection, effective casting, and line management all play an important part of a successful strategy.

That strategy might be described as: "From a distance or location offering concealment, cast your selected fly very close to the undercut bank, allowing the fly to drift along that bank with no drag." In those situations where a bubble line is present, try to place your fly in the bubble line or, even better, between it and the bank. Your fly must appear both natural and easy to capture to the trout for best results. Well, that may take some practice, huh!

Smooth runs hold fish when they are feeding but probably not when they are hiding unless they are quite deep. Perhaps this is because the fish can see food moving toward them, and they can watch out for predators with relatively little distortion within the constraints of their sight geometry. Trout in shallow smooth runs are generally very spooky. The key

challenges for fishermen are to stay out of the trout's view and to present the fly with no tell-tale drag. This might be the place to tie on a finer tippet. The smooth surface of runs are a perfect canvas upon which to paint little wakes from your fly. And, of course, it's easy to see the spooked trout leave a smooth run, too. If you "line" the trout closest to you, you can watch all the trout seek cover.

Beaver Ponds can hold some surprising fish. More recently formed ponds seem to harbor better (but perhaps fewer) fish than older ones, possibly due to over population and limited food supply in older ponds. All of them warrant investigation. Most are difficult to get to; after all the beaver makes them to flood their selected area. This leads to marsh and prolific brush. Trout in beaver ponds are notoriously spooky, therefore your approach must be very stealthy if you are to be very successful. The best water in a beaver pond is likely to be where the stream enters the pond, the deepest area in the pond and where the water

exits the pond. The deepest area is generally at the dam but can be in holes along the original stream bed. Frequently the challenge to fishing a beaver pond is simply getting a fly to likely water, so a careful scout around the pond can pay handsome dividends. Don't overlook an approach straight up the stream to the dam itself. This can offer access to deeper water, concealment behind the dam as well as an opening for your back cast. The downside is trying to land a fish with your line tangled in the sticks and logs of the dam.

Rising/feeding trout are the best! Casting to a visible, actively feeding fish and being able to see it take your fly, then bringing it to hand is one of the most rewarding thrills of fly fishing! Clearly it's one of the most important reasons we so enjoy fly fishing small streams. They are shallow and so often offer the opportunity of "sight fishing!" We get some immediate and candid feedback on our fishing skills, too, in this situation. In small streams the fisherman can not only see the rise forms of trout feeding at the surface and near-surface of the water, but frequently

also fish feeding on nymphs and such near the stream's bottom. A key challenge to the fisherman here is to place the appropriate fly in the water close enough to be noticed by the feeding fish. If your target is a fish feeding on the surface, you must place your fly, drifting naturally, closer to the fish in shallow water than in deeper water. Remember the nature of the fish's "vision cone." In six inches of water the fish can see on the water's surface a circle of only about twelve to fourteen inches in diameter. From a depth of twelve inches, a fish can see a circle of over twenty-four inches in diameter. And also remember the rise form is generally not directly above the fish's lie, but somewhat downstream from where you saw the rise form. How much downstream is dependent on how far below the water surface the trout is holding and how swift the water is. When feeding on nymphs, a fish has substantially fewer vision restrictions. The primary factor in this case is probably how far the fish will move to intercept a likely food item, ie., how profitable will the morsel be if the fish eats it. Here again it appears reasonable that the closer the attractive fly is to the fish, the more likely it is to be eaten. A challenge to the fisherman is to account for the distortion of light as it enters water from the atmosphere and thus where the fish actually lies versus where it appears to lie. Depending on the angle at which you view the fish and its depth in the water, it can appear to be quite a bit ahead of its actual position. Of course this phenomenon can influence your efforts for an effective drift of your fly.

Unusual lies

One of the many reasons we just don't get tired of fishing for trout in small streams is that they, the trout, surprise us so often. Sometimes they ain't where they are supposed to be and sometimes they are where they're not supposed to be. Here's a few examples of places that, in our experience, have held unexpected trout. By the way; the dark area in the lower left of the image on the next page is a boot belonging to one of your authors. Just happened to look down and there it was! The trout, that is.

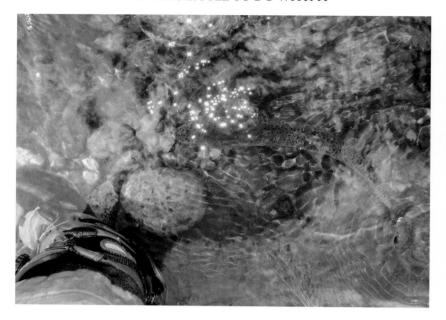

Very shallow water. Really, hardly enough water to cover the trout's back. Why are the trout there? Warming up in the sun? Found more nymphs in the warmer shallow water? Who knows; but it might pay to drop a fly in that "too shallow" water just to see what happens. But don't try to get too close; these trout know they are exposed and they are really spooky.

Just downstream from a trail crossing. Probably the trout were enjoying some nice nymphs kicked up by passing hikers, fishermen, or bears, all on their way to someplace else. Since these trout seem more adapted to traffic near them, they are less likely to spook for long when you or your partner comes by. If you've a little patience, this can set up a really great tale at the end of the day! "Ed just walked right by that fifteen inch fish! Can you imagine?"

A depression too small to hold the trout it did. At least it seemed that way. More than once we've scared a trout out of a spot too small to hold it. Of course, that fish scooting up the stream spooked others on the way to its safer hiding place. There is really no good substitute for careful observation and slow movement while going up a small stream, whether you are on the bank or in the water.

Isolated Pools left by dropping water. We've taken fish from these and put them back in the main flow. Felt good to do that. But it might be illegal. Of course you could apply for a permit. On second thought, it really wasn't one of us; we just heard about it.

Chapter Nine
The Last Foot: Landing That
Unexpected Large Trout

"It is not a fish until it is on the bank"
Irish proverb

It can happen in any number of ways. On your first cast, when you're just shaken' out the coils in your line. After you are lulled by catching several eight inch Brookies. When you are distracted by elk coming out of the woods... You're distracted, no matter how. Wham! A fifteen inch trout, or larger even, strikes and (probably) sets the hook herself. Or maybe you were, intentionally, prepared for this big fish 'cause you saw it! No matter; when we get truly and extra excited by the trout on our line, things can take a strange turn.

It's easy to say, "When the unexpected occurs, just stay calm." But we wouldn't say that; how could we take the easy way out and collect the handsome royalties on this fine book? Also, do we enjoy fishing small streams because we have perfect emotional control? No. No more than we can hook a fine fish, only to lose it, with calm acceptance.

Sometimes, somehow, the big one just breaks off. How else does the legend of "the one that got away" get started – even among really good anglers. You might think small streams are less prone to offer a situation leading to losing a good fish, but our experience suggests otherwise. Only the surprise is bigger.

There are lots of things we can do to turn that legend into a photo of the trophy trout. Lots of our advice is common to good fishing habits anywhere. Things like tying appropriate knots well, keeping your equipment in good condition, managing your fly line so it doesn't tangle about your feet or around stuff on the ground, checking tippet for "wind knots" and abrasion, etc.. There are a few points we think are especially important to successful small stream fishing. Keeping in mind that the space you have to play and land a fish in a small stream is, itself, small, we think unnecessarily light tippets are unwise. That nice fish won't have to go far to the nearest root snag, bank overhang, or sharp rock – ping! You lose more flies in the brush with fine tippets, too. Fishing in the typical shallow water and rocks of small streams and tussling with their stream side brush can damage tippets fast. So can high winds combined with short, fast casts. Therefore checking and replacing them frequently is a good investment of your on stream time. Also especially important is line control; fish in close quarters seem to be quite adept at taking advantage of even a little bit of extra slack in the line. You are fishing barbless, aren't you?

As alluded to above, it doesn't take long to get into trouble when landing a nice fish in a small stream; they just don't have far to go to break off on rocks, roots, and such. This places a premium on controlling the fish; allowing the trout "room to fight" or to make (relatively) long runs will reduce your chances of landing it. On the other hand bringing a nice fish quickly to hand or net creates its own set of problems. Some trout might flip the hook from its mouth into your hand or worse, your face, and can really hurt you. Other situations, such as the trout flopping about on the rocks at your feet, can hurt the fish. Sometimes a good trout will flip the hook out right at your feet – the classic "quick release" some of us are wont to claim. None of these are ideal for the later story told to your friends.

So what's the fortunate angler to do? Well, folks, "the basics" are called the basics for good reason. But recalling them while justifiably excited is a challenge. Experience (in losing good fish) helps you recall those basics at the right time but such experience is frustrating to say the least! Here are some things that will help you land that fish without going through the school of hard knocks. Think about them and practice them on all the fish you hook and they'll be there for you when you really need them for the Big One. First, don't give the fish any slack. Second, allow the fish to tire on a modest amount of line. Third, keep your rod tip lower than most fishing photos show. If you hold your rod tip very high how will you keep slack out of the line if the fish swims toward you? Think you can strip line fast enough? We think it best to keep your fly rod at about a forty-five degree angle to the water's surface. This allows two very important things to happen. You can still react rapidly to a fish charging you and you avoid fighting the fish from your rod's tip; that is, you can use all the rod to fight the fish and avoid breaking your light rod's tip section. Fourth, try to keep the fish working against both your line and across the stream current; that is, don't let him swim directly upstream or downstream. Turn his head to make him swim across the current to tire him more quickly. Fifth; as you bring your big trout in close it will see you and try to run. Let it; but on a snug line. If you've retrieved line on the reel (and you better have: see Chapter Seven!) let your properly set drag do this work; if not, hope you can let out line smoothly between your fingers and hope it doesn't tangle up on your feet or rocks, branches, and such. Repeat step number five until the trout is yours, but don't overdo the fight as you can easily tire the fish too much and kill it. After freeing your hook, carefully, lightly, hold the fish in its normal upright orientation and move it back and forth in the stream current to rest and revive it, then let it swim out of your hands in its own good time.

Other tips include not moving your rod tip when you wind in line to your reel during the fight (no slack, remember?) A good fish will frequently swim quickly and directly toward you – be prepared (no slack, remember?) Rainbows, and sometimes other trout, will leap from the water to try to throw your fly. While the leap is beautiful and dramatic and exciting and its own reward, it's also frequently a winning strategy for the trout. Most experts recommend dipping your rod tip or "bowing" to the trout when it leaps in order to purposefully introduce a slight amount of slack in your line and so keep the trout connected. We think this helps but is no guarantee. It seems trout leaping is a great strategy for the trout. Maybe we should say "no accidental slack," huh? Smart (agitated?) trout like to go for rocks, branches, and other obstacles in the water during the fight. While you might lose the trout by forcing it away from those obstacles, you are likely to lose her if she

gets to them. You make the decision.

Finally, we strongly favor losing a good trout trying to land it rather than playing it to death, don't you?

Chapter Ten

Small Streams and Kids

"In my family, there was no clear division between religion and fly fishing."
Norman Maclean, A River Runs Through It, 1976

Some of our favorite partners on small streams are children. We can't think of better "quality time" with children. They generally are eager to learn, quick to imitate successful on-stream behaviors, and truly excited when things go well. They are not much burdened by either past success or failure. The stream is different and they instinctively know it. It's smaller and it fits 'em! They are quick to forgive and forget errors – theirs and yours. They get along very well with a minimum of equipment and the accessories apparently so necessary to the adult fly fishing "expert." On the other hand, as the above image shows, kids like "stuff," too and it can help encourage them to the stream. Not much gets in the way of their fun, and that's as it should be. They are focused - but you must aim them. Unexpected problems with aim might come up, especially with younger kids. That is, they might forget what they are on stream for and prefer to chase grasshoppers rather than catch fish. How do you compete with grasshoppers? Something that works for us is to hook a fish, then hand the rod to them. If they land the fish, they want to try again; if they lose the fish, they want to try again, same as you.

Another way to aim a smaller or beginning child's interest on stream is to show them a likely lie for fish, then catch one from that lie. They'll start watching for another such place and you can begin to teach them how to "read the water." They'll start showing you where the fish are in no time flat! This works even if our burgeoning young fisherman isn't in the mood to fish that day. And they'll want to come back again.

Small streams offer small beginning anglers and small developing anglers a truly special place in which to grow (and not only in fly fishing skills). Merely by their size, small streams are less intimidating to kids. Everything that is present on large waters is present here; just in smaller, more concentrated, and more visible amounts. It's safe to say these streams are obvious rather than subtle in their characteristics. This makes it easier for novice and young angler alike to see everything they need to see about the fishing environment, all in one glance. They can see pools, riffles, current seams, bends, undercut banks, gravel beaches, runs, cover, etc., all together. And all must go together in order to make our book title accurate. Otherwise fly fishing's a crap shoot.

Small streams require less skill to catch the first trout and more to catch the best trout. You may quote us on this.

As mentioned above, less equipment is required – you just

need a light rod, line and only a few flies to taste success. Maybe only one fly; a size twelve or fourteen Parachute Adams or Elk Hair Caddis will do very well, indeed. Waders are unnecessary since generally there is little need to step into the water. Fly vest? Tools and spools? Why? Consider the advantages of you carrying all that stuff. You have it anyway and being the supply center facilitates your ongoing assistance to the young angler. On the other hand some young anglers want to dress like their mentor. Don't wait 'till you get to the stream to find out. We do, however, always recommend one item of specialized equipment – a pair of polarized sunglasses. More on that later.

The young angler's casting skills need not be well developed for them to be successful. Remember, a couple of chapters back we said one small stream skill can frequently be compensated for by another. Kids play hide and seek all the time; stealth and concealment come naturally to them. They love to crawl around and can get on their knees and belly a lot easier than we adults. So encourage them to do what they enjoy and do best. Don't worry; as they get older they'll see the advantages of good casting skills and soon they'll begin to out-fish you. Ready for that? Maybe you want to remain their fishing hero just a while longer. Speaking of being their hero, know that they are watching you even more than you think, and learning – good or bad. One of our grandchildren learned the slingshot cast by watching his grandfather, without granddad knowing it. The seven year old was supposed to be just dragging a nymph through a likely hole on his own while his grandfather was fishing the next spot upstream. Granddad wasn't aware of being watched until the youngster yelled in delight upon catching a Brookie from under a willow overhanging the stream. It was one of the first trout caught entirely on his own and he was rightfully proud of both the fish and the way he caught it.

Small streams are really great teaching labs for kids. They provide nearly immediate feedback on everything one does; right or wrong. This is why we recommend polarized sunglasses for kids on stream. Of course they will think they look cool, but that's not the point. With polarized sunglasses, they can see into the water much more clearly and when they rush up to the stream bank to begin fishing, you don't have to holler, "Don't run; you'll spook the fish." They themselves can see the fish bolt to cover. Now, if you say (calmly), "Don't run; you'll spook the fish" at the same time they see the fish bolt to cover, they will think you know a lot about fishing. Then later, when you have other fly fishing pearls of wisdom to share with them, they might listen. That is good.

While we're not academic experts on teaching techniques for kids we do realize they are not all alike in the way they learn. Some don't want to try for themselves until they are real comfortable with what's expected and what to expect and how it's done and so on. Some want to grab a rod and rush the stream. Most fall somewhere in between and all are willing to try in proportion to their trust of you. And of course age and attention span considerations fall in there as well. Keep it fun, by their definition, and

neither of you will be disappointed in small stream fly fishing, whether you catch fish or not.

At some point they will need to "fish on their own;" without your help and advice. In this endeavor their success will inspire them and their problems will set up the next opportunity for you to help. So we recommend you give 'em space but watch that they don't get too frustrated. At first you might have to offer assistance because they don't know what they're doing wrong but later they'll let you know when they're ready for you to help. A final word on the advantages of small streams for developing fishing skills in kids. Mostly small streams are shallow, so when a child falls (or jumps) into one, they are probably not in serious danger, although it may sound like it. Most small streams are cold.

The last paragraph in no way relieves you of your responsibility for the safety of a child when you fish with them. Best you take that very seriously.

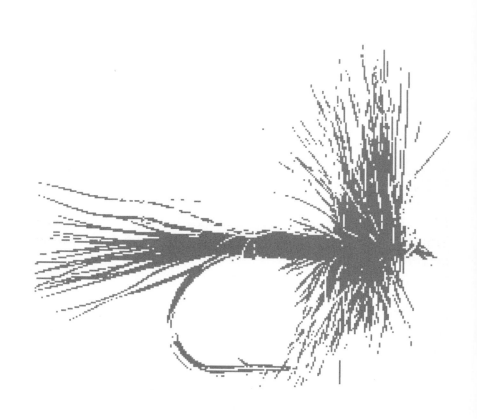

Chapter Eleven
Small Stream Trout
and Their Habits

"Angling may be said to be so like the mathematics
that it can never be fully learnt."
Izaak Walton, *The Compleat Angler* (1653)

Small streams, especially in the Rockies, support a wonderful variety of wild trout. Wild, because generally these streams are too small to warrant stocking, at least not recently. Nice. The skilled fisherman can encounter Brook Trout, Cutthroat Trout, Rainbow Trout, Cuttbow Trout, Brown Trout, Apache Trout and other species of trout, as well as other cold water fish while angling in mountain streams. We won't try to be a comprehensive reference for these fish but some comments on the identification and habits of the most common trout will be very helpful to the small stream fisherman. As an aside, the trout illustrated here were all caught by the authors in small Rocky Mountain streams. Our usual priority is to return fish caught in these streams to the water as quickly as possible so you might reasonably find flaws in our photography. All of the fish pictured here were successfully returned alive and active to their stream.

Brook Trout; native to the eastern United States and perhaps the most commonly encountered trout (really, a char rather than a trout) in small streams is easily identified by its dark green back with verticules and orange fins tipped in white. Red spots surrounded by blue also occur on their sides. They were widely introduced into cold waters most everywhere in the U.S. beginning over 200 years ago. They are prolific, quick to mature, and relatively short-lived in small streams. Brook trout prefer quiet water near the more swift currents that will bring them food.

Cutthroat Trout are found most often in very high elevation mountain streams. They are native to the western U.S. but do not compete well with other trout, so generally a barrier to upstream migration establishes their most downstream occurrence. Over a dozen subspecies of Cutthroats have been reported in previous publications. Their appearance varies with their native habitat but all have distinct spots on their sides, especially toward the tail, against a yellowish background. They also have bright red to orange slashes under their jaw. The photo above depicts a Rio Grande Cutthroat, caught, as appropriate, from somewhere in the headwaters of the Rio Grande River. All these trout should be immediately returned to the stream since most are at least fairly rare. But the good news is that they are hard to get to. Long walks at high elevations and such.

Rainbow Trout, native to West Coast watersheds, were widely introduced into other cold water streams worldwide. Wild Rainbows have declined rapidly in U.S. streams, especially in the West, over the past twenty years. The decline is due to Whirling Disease, which affects their fry. Some disease-resistant Rainbows have been re-introduced into selected Western rivers where it is hoped they will reproduce, but they are not often found in small streams. They are a wonderful trout that like to leap when caught and prefer faster water when in streams. Adult hatchery raised Rainbows are widely stocked in suitable waters.

Cuttbow trout, a cross between Cutthroat and Rainbow trout have been introduced to many western watersheds, have thrived, and can be commonly found in high mountain streams. They are a beautiful trout that sometimes doesn't get the respect it deserves. They are not shy around food (even if it's artificial) and fight well. These trout vary substantially in coloration, spot distribution, etc. perhaps due to their parent cutthroat or maybe the rock coloration in the bed of their home stream, or both. They will have that orange or red slash under their jaw characteristic of Cutthroat Trout and probably the hint of a pink stripe down their lateral line.

Brown Trout, of course, were imported from Europe a long time ago. They no longer know it and have no discernible accent at all. Some say Brown trout are the "smartest" and most difficult trout to catch, but some of us think that idea got started because Browns, especially large ones, like subdued light and most folks don't like to fish at night. Or under logs and other under water cover where it is easy to lose a fly.

In any case they can and do migrate up small streams from larger waters, where they were once (or still are) stocked, to spawn. Some must like the environment because we've caught them in small waters during times they weren't supposed to be spawning.

Brown Trout can get really large as they are prone to eat other fish. Thus the small stream angler can be very pleasantly surprised if they are skilled enough to catch one.

Splake, the hybrid of a male Brook Trout and a female Lake Trout has been around as a stocked fish since the early 1880s but they are seldom seen in small streams. They are sometimes known as "Wendigo"- really! We read up on this after catching a few in small Rocky Mountain streams. Although the image shown here was chosen for its obvious difference in appearance from either hybrid parent, markings and coloration seem to vary even more widely than Cuttbow and sometimes they can be easily mistaken for a Brook Trout. The experts say look for a "V" in their tails in comparison to the "square tailed" Brook Trout. Splake are perhaps more common in Eastern waters than in Western and then mostly in lakes. However if the small stream you're fishing empties directly into or originates in a stocked lake you might catch one of these and think you've got an award-winning Brook

Trout. They are known to exhibit more rapid growth than either parent species and have been reported to be capable of reaching a length of eighteen inches in two years, under ideal conditions. According to the literature, Splake are considered easier to catch than other trout and char, but if you latch on to a sixteen inch Splake in a small stream you might form your own opinion. By "catch" we mean "land," of course; all fishing records would be different if anglers counted merely hooking a fish. Discussion around the campfire notwithstanding.

Chapter Twelve
Equipment

"The man who coined the phrase 'Money can't buy happiness' never bought himself a good fly rod!"
Reg Baird, from his video, *Labrador Trout*

There are some really fine books and catalogs devoted to fishing equipment for most any occasion and we don't want to compete with them. That being said, we think it's true that small streams, especially those off the beaten path, require a bit of consideration equipment-wise for safety, comfort and success. Many good streams will be in the backcountry or even in wilderness areas, a long walk from civilized food, water, and shelter. So you are advised to take your own. Even on a short trip taking something for lunch is a good idea and there is an abundance of excellent trail worthy foods available. Just choose your favorite. We suggest you take along plenty of safe water as water from the streams you fish might contain unhealthy organisms such as Guardia. Alternately you might consider a filtration pump or UV light "pen" marketed to purify water. We don't claim these to be effective or not, on advice of our in-house lawyer, but check 'em out and make your own decision. A good hat and rain jacket are very welcome during the frequent afternoon rain (or sleet, snow, or gropple) which occurs in the high mountains during the summer months. You must also take personal responsibility for your own first aid and medical needs. Simple and light is key.

If you plan to do much back country angling you may want to consider purchase of an emergency global positioning device capable of alerting appropriate folks via satellite if you get into real trouble with no help around. These things are relatively inexpensive and are capable of alerting the local Search and Rescue officials that you are immobilized by a true emergency and of your exact location. By pushing a different button, they can also be used to reassure someone that you're just running late, and are not injured. This feature helps some of us stay on the right side of our spouses.

Be optimistic; carry a camera. Current camera technology is nothing short of amazing! Even awesome! Several manufacturers have models designed for outdoor sport use. The interested can obtain really rugged cameras water proof to ten or more feet, shock proof for a five foot drop on a rock, with a global positioning device built in, maybe even a calculator and phone, as well. And they take superb images, too. And can store hundreds of photos to be downloaded to your computer or played on the camera screen or on your home or camp television. This might even give one the capability to "photo shop" your trophy, (We don't really know exactly what "photo shop" is but it sounds dishonest and thus we do not recommend it.) Seriously, a good camera is a real treat to have on your fishing expedition, essential to your angling credibility, credentials as an artist, and just plain fun. Many excellent ones can be operated with one hand leaving the other free to manage the trout properly. It's possible a good camera is the best few ounces you carry along with your rod and reel.

Fishing equipment is pretty basic. A three, four or five weight fly rod and reel will be the ideal choice. Heavier fly fishing gear or spin or casting gear is unnecessary and inappropriate. Small stream trout deserve to be taken on barbless flies delivered via a fly rod. Do not argue on this point lest your reputation as an angler be tarnished, if not destroyed completely. While a spirited discussion can ensue when choosing rod length; we suggest shorter rods, eight feet or less. Short fly rods are easier to handle in brush while longer rods perform better in high winds. Some compromise will be necessary since it's impractical to cart several rods and associated equipment along on a hike. A three piece rod in a case provides a neat package to strap on your pack. Anticipated fish size and/or weather conditions will help you choose amongst the suggested fly fishing gear. Your choice of rod is very important. It should not be too stiff; it must load with only a small amount of line beyond the tip top and be sensitive without sloppiness. While graphite rods are excellent in longer lengths and heavier weights, many tend to be mediocre in short, light versions. They are insensitive and insulate the fisherman from the lively and colorful trout often found in small mountain streams. Most fiberglass rods, other than those made from S-glass, tend to be too slow and sloppy. Bamboo rods, on the other hand, are ideal; having the ability to load with a minimum of line out as well as handle longer casts if required. They are sensitive and well known for protecting fine tippets. They also lend an air of respect and elegance to the small stream fishing experience. Plus they are beautiful; even works of art. It's a well known fact that trout caught on a fine handcrafted bamboo fly rod are less chagrined than those caught on more pedestrian rods mass-produced from graphite or fiberglass. Bamboo fly rods also look good in your photos/images and just owning one or more enhances your reputation. If the cost of a custom bamboo fly rod is a real obstacle, please refer again to the chapter quote. Some of us think they are worth saving up for.

Local conditions will dictate choice of fly patterns but you shouldn't need more than five or six dry patterns and as many nymphs and/or streamers. Reliable dry fly standbys include the Parachute Adams, Elk Hair Caddis, Stimulators and Humpys in sizes twelve and fourteen. We like beadhead nymphs for shallow waters; they get down but, in sizes fourteen to eighteen, are not apt to hang up on the bottom structure as much as more heavily weighted flies. Prince, Pheasant Tail and Copper Johns work well, as do a number of other caddis and mayfly emulators. The progress of the growing season and the resulting insect hatches will guide you in selection, color and size. The authors don't get up tight about specific flies for small stream angling. We know two very successful small stream anglers who fish almost exclusively with a single fly pattern; one fishes a Parachute Adams and another fishes an Elk Hair Caddis.

One of our backpacking buddies has been known to go through his hiking partners' backpacks throwing out "unnecessary" stuff before an adventure. The principle is great; the execution risky. But keep it simple and light so you can walk farther.

You've seen a dog in several of the pictures in this book, including at the front of this chapter. What about taking a dog on your fly fishing trip? Don't they jump into the water, get tangled in the fly line, and otherwise disrupt fishing? Well, we asked one pictured dog's owner and here's what he said:

Does a dog belong on a Fishing Trip?

The guide member in this author group has strong opinions on dogs and wilderness fly fishing! A well trained dog is good to have in the back country, it keeps you aware of the things in your surroundings that you may have missed and they are great companions. A dog was not part of the guide team the first few years that I provided guide service in the wilderness. After a particularly tough trip into a remote stream I began to change my thoughts about having a dog along when the customer said, "Did you notice all the wild game tracks in there?" We had seen all kinds of tracks including bear and cat, but, so what; we had caught a lot of fish so I thought things were great. He said that was scary. The next morning he stopped by the trailer and gave me a leash, saying next year you should have a dog on that leash. He followed that up with "a well trained dog alerts you and the customer of possible trouble ahead." I knew he was a dog trainer so I asked if it should be one of his bird dogs, he responded with "wrong kind of dog for this job." You need a dog with the following traits:

- Strong loyalty to one person,
- Sticks close, does not go off hunting,
- Tough,
- Tenacious,
- Trainable,
- Will swim, but is not naturally drawn to swim.

You need a cow dog! Aka Australian cattle dog or blue or red heeler. Now I am not saying a cow dog is the only choice because many breeds can be trained to do the job, but a cow dog with good breeding comes equipped with most of the traits you need. You just need to spend time with it so it knows what you want and when. Make sure that you establish that you are the leader of the pack. Teach it what a leash is about, how to heel, when to whoa and sit. Voice and hand commands are important. After leash training is mastered it is time to go off leash. To get the dog to stay close, just go somewhere that has lots of distractions and things for you to hide behind. Start walking with the dog off leash, as soon as it starts wandering or not paying attention to you, step behind something. The dog will sense that you are not there and begin to look for you, It will get nervous. Step back out where it can see you. The dog will have a relieved look and come running to you. After a few times of losing sight of you the dog will keep an eye on you while accomplishing the task at hand. A cow dog will learn what you want by just being around you whether in the home or the field. Like any dog it just wants to please the pack leader.

Dogs are wonderful companions anywhere and anytime. One of my favorite things to do is sit down overlooking a stream and watch the fish. There are many pictures, taken by customers, of me doing this and my dog Willow will be sitting behind me watching my back. If she begins a low growl I know we have company and I had better see what is coming our way, could be people or wild life. Another story that happened years ago may carry companionship just a too little to far. I took a lady, her son, and her grandson into a remote site, five hours on horseback to get there, for a three day two night trip. About thirty minutes after the wrangler and the horses headed back I realized that I had left the sleeping bags in the back seat of my truck! I guess I had a strange look on my face, because the lady asked "is there something wrong." I just smiled and said, oh I left the sleeping bags in the truck but we will be just fine. I went ahead setting up camp using rain flies, canvas from my bed roll and the extra fleece bags that I was carrying in my duffel to make their beds. When it was time to go to bed I went to my tent, put on my rain slicker, laid down on the ground and pulled Willow in with me. You have probably heard of three dog nights, well, for next two nights one dog would have to do!

A well trained dog is essential to the successful wilderness fly fishing trip.

Chapter 13
On-Stream Behavior and Etiquette

*"There is certainly something in fishing that tends to produce
a gentleness of spirit, a pure serenity of mind"*
Washington Irving (1783 - 1859)

In this era of increasingly callous and selfish (it's all about me) "adult" behavior, small stream fly fishing can offer a refreshing respite. Most "fishermen" with poor attitudes and behaviors won't put in the effort you and I will to secure a special fishing experience, simply because they don't take much responsibility for their own actions or lack of action in any aspect of their lives, never mind fishing. In short, they are lazy – physically, morally, and ethically. While it's clear we don't care for this type of "fisherman," it's also generally true that they don't much populate our favorite streams, except when they are very close to a road or accessible by ATV (either legally or illegally).

Of course some of these "fishermen" are simply ignorant; that is, they are unaware of the proper behaviors on stream. It is to these teachable fishermen that this chapter is dedicated. Present company excepted, but you may be called to loan your copy of this book to someone else as an act of kindness. Of course, if they learn the right attitude and behavior from this chapter, they'll need their own copy of the book for reference. If they don't seem to get it, please retrieve your loaned copy (if they admit to still having it) and don't say anything else about its content. Maybe they'll forget the other lessons herein.

You might well ask "How can you guys set yourself up as judges of on-stream behavior? Well, need we remind you one of us is a Judge (retired) with over forty years fly fishing experience? The other two of us are also experienced fly fishermen with well-balanced moral and ethical compasses. That ought to do 'till something better comes along.

No surprise. The Golden Rule (you know; the one that says "Do unto others as you would have them do unto you") is really all you need to know and practice while fly fishing small streams. At the same time some specifics pertaining to small stream situations can be helpful.

"Enough space" on a small stream means something different than it does on a popular Eastern river. Space is likely the most volatile of any small stream etiquette situation and probably a concept best negotiated personally with the fisherman you have just encountered on the small stream. Consider the possibility that there is only room for one of you on this little Brookie stream and you have to walk a bit further to another stream or come back another day. He got there first, didn't he?

Take extra care not to spook fish in the area someone else is fishing or will fish in the next half hour or so. Remember how shy these fish are.

Be respectful of the fisherman that has just arrived. Maybe he didn't know enough about the long, hard trail to start early. Or perhaps standards are different in their area. Invite him or her to share the water, if possible. Keep in mind there's more glory in catching fish from water someone else has already fished than them catching trout from water you've just fished through. If several new fishermen show up on "your stream" remind them of the Golden Rule. If they insist or push, consider shooting one as an example. Of course we don't recommend you actually do shoot someone; just consider it for venting purposes and to re-establish your own priorities. Consider the bigger picture; there might be an electrical storm over this stream soon.

Nature calls. But be modest about it. You may only think you're alone.

The person you encounter on a small stream may not be interested in (or knowledgeable about) fishing. Maybe this is good; maybe not. Here's another opportunity to strike up a conversation and decide how ya'll won't interfere with each other.

In all interactions keep in mind it's unlawful to deny anyone fishing access to public water flowing thru public lands.

Chapter 14
Where Are These Wonderful Small Streams?

"Few people who travel in Ireland are fully aware of its beauties, for in good truth they are not to be seen by traveling along the high road: they lie hid on the shores of the lakes and the banks of the rivers: they must be sought for on foot, or discovered by accident."-

The Rev. Henry Newland, *The Erne, its Legends and its Fly-Fishing* (1851)

This chapter has been left to near the end of the book on purpose because, up until now, you couldn't be trusted with the information. But you've now been exposed to some of the philosophy, as well as science, of small stream angling; even so, we are taking a calculated risk. Don't disappoint us.

Most of the best small streams are in the mountains – high up. And not generally accessible by car. Many have trails to or along side them, but not all. Most all of them are out of sight from a road, or at least the segment in which you are interested is. Almost all of them take some real effort and time to get to. Most require work to access and enjoy. Discouraged? Good; so are most people. And thus the rest of us get to better enjoy some of God's greatest accomplishments on this earth. We feel "nothing ventured; nothing gained" really applies to small streams. Now, that's something to celebrate, because men and women of good character enjoy nothing so much as a thing well earned.

But on to the question. By far the best way to find these little gems on your own is to study maps. A good map with topographical information will show you the stream, its gradient and how to get to it. Sometimes it will show trails; sometimes not. Of course things can look different once you get on site; but that's what scouting is all about, isn't it? What type of water are you looking for? A personal favorite is a meadow with stream oxbows thru it. Some like pocket water better. The map will reveal these characteristics, or at least imply them, via topographical gradient information. What it will not show is the size and depth of the stream and how brush choked it is. Water depth is important because the trout must be able to winter over and need those holes to do it in. The importance of brush is obvious. So it's possible to find a shallow, brush choked and barren stream at the end of a several mile hike uphill. But it will be a nice trip anyway. And you can selectively reveal that location to… well, you decide that.

A sometimes reliable way to find good streams is to ask someone knowledgeable. The local fly shop is often an excellent source of information and you'll get the same information as dozens of other anglers. These folks stay in business by helping anglers succeed and there's sure nothing wrong with that! To get guidance on those special little known streams you'll need to find out from the local private experts. But you've got to be careful with this one. Lots of fishermen think each angler should find their own "best fish'n hole" unless invited otherwise. Maybe a better way is to just listen… quietly…and respectfully, if you're fortunate enough to be around any of those experts. And don't rush it, either. Wasn't it Yogi Berra that said "you can hear a lot just by listening?" We recommend pleasant surroundings and maybe a libation to facilitate camaraderie. For example, one of your authors enjoys fine bourbon; the Judge will have a beer from time to time, and the guide is so polite he'll drink most anything you have. You can figure out what your favorite "knowledgeable person" enjoys. Lots of fishermen like to talk about their fishing trips in the presence of those that are interested. Be interested and subtle. This is not the time for an interrogation nor a "biggest lie" competition but leading questions are generally allowed. Of course you must have your BS meter turned on. We find the most modest fishermen are the most reliable ones, present company excepted.

With luck and a pleasant disposition you might even be invited to partake of that special stream. We should warn you that such an invitation comes with a caveat; you must keep confidential that which you learn from a truly good source of fishing locations. If you blab the "secret location" or if you invite another along on the trip to a "secret location" you risk being exempted from further participation. No, your knowledgeable source doesn't own the stream and, with today's maps, GPS and computer mapping programs, there are few, if any, unknown streams in the U.S. Your source does, however, have specific, valid, and probably recent on-site experience with the stream in question, and they have put in the "sweat equity" to gain that information. And it's his to share – or not. Best you respect that. Who knows; you may be tested. Some pass and some fail; guess who has the most fun?

Which brings up another suggestion; namely, hire a guide. But that costs money, you say. Well, please decide what you are after; your purpose, your objective. Do you want to fish, or cut bait? What's a special fishing experience worth in dollars, anyway?

Sometimes we don't have the time due to work, family obligations, etc. or maybe you have little interest in the "do it yourself" approach. If that's the case hiring a knowledgeable guide is by far the best way to find a good stream for the simple reason that he is interested in maintaining his reputation. In addition, the good ones truly enjoy seeing "their" anglers be successful on the stream. Most of the time hiring a good guide encompasses another excellent benefit, too: a coach. You still have to read this book, mind you, but having a coach nearby to help you apply these suggestions will accelerate your learning curve and result in more fish and more fun in very short order! The only caveat attached to the guide suggestion is to ensure your prospective guide is truly knowledgeable about your target area and that he or she is truly knowledgeable about small stream fishing. The latter is especially easy to determine since you can formulate test questions from this book.

What follows is a report of a "scout" by a crusty old guide into the wilderness in search of wild trout. It is presented as stated; with only a little clean-up to help suppress profanity:

Hunting Wild Trout

The hunt for wild trout is not always easy and is often time consuming. First let's understand what we mean by a "wild trout" as not everyone has the same definition. To some of us it is a group of fish in an area of water that has not been stocked in the last ten years and stocked fish from other areas can not get to the area because of waterfalls or other similar barrier. To be specific, I am more interested in wild Rio Grande Cutthroat, the only native trout to the upper Rio Grande watershed. There are books available today that say the wildlife (including fish) status in this area was almost non-existent in the early 1900s due to the demand for food and the tourist pressure. Many of the local ranchers began restocking programs in local and remote waters, several developed fish farming programs. One source of this information is "Crusaders for Wildlife." (ed. See the bibliography.)

The hunt can be broken down into three steps. #1 Finding locations where wild trout could exist. #2 Putting together the equipment that will be needed. #3 Last but not least, getting your group in shape to make the trip. Locations are found by getting general maps of the area you are interested in scouting. Look for areas that have remote streams, waterfalls, and not many trails. When you have an area identified with these attributes get detailed maps (topographical maps) of the area. The topographical maps may reveal any terrain conditions that could restrict stocked fish from moving up the stream to this area. Now that you have found an area you are interested in scouting, review your group's backcountry skill set and physical condition to make sure the group is up to the challenge. Altitude and changes in the altitude may be some of the biggest factors to consider, but there are many more challenges you need to think about. Such as can you use a map and compass to find your location along a trail, can you read the weather and do you have a SPOT and GPS? If you have doubts, get into a training class. Where you are going there will be no one to help you! A well trained dog is always good to have along, they are much more aware of other animals that you may not have noticed. You should always have another person along with good skills and in shape. The only drawback is that when you get back to your truck or maybe while still in the wilderness you will need to kill him to protect your find! HA! Take extra food, one extra days worth for a four day trip. The more prepared you are, the easier it will be to remain cool and collected under strained situations. Next get your gear together. Whatever you do, don't go on an exploring trip with a pack you can't easily carry over tough terrain and in bad weather. Ask a friend who has some backpacking experience to review your gear for additions and reductions. Keep in mind, you are not on a luxury trip; you will be roughing it. OK, let's go find the fish! Stop by the local ranger station to let them know where you are going and when you expect to be out. This is important in case something were to happen on the trip. When you get to the trail head also sign in and remember to sign out when you return. It is part of being safe and it also allows the forest service to know how much use a trail or area is receiving. Alright, lets move out, steady and easy, no sense in killing yourself two hours into a four or five day trip. This may be a new environment for your dog; check it out. Drink plenty of water. We use an UV pen to treat the drinking water, seems to work well and it is lightweight and quick.

Fishing a wild trout stream is different than fishing the streams near campgrounds and towns because they don't get the traffic from fishermen. However, they also may be grown over, making traditional casting impossible. That is when casts like the steeple, bow, and spey are important to know.

Your fly selection is not as important, most of the time the fish will try anything that looks like food. But always have plenty of hoppers, nymphs, Stimulators, and Adams with you. Remember from previous chapters about how to approach the stream. Choose a nice secluded spot for your camp; no sense telling the world where you are. Even though this kind of place does not have many trails and is not talked about much there may be others like you searching for the hidden pockets of wild trout. It is also important to camp without leaving a trace of your being there: just another part of being on a wild trout stream. Remember, if you want it to stay good for future trips, the fewer fishermen you tell about it the less visits it will receive! See Chapter Fifteen for more on this philosophy.

The last scouting trip we took was very rewarding. We located a very nice stretch of stream about four miles in length with good sized cutthroats. We camped in a great location with good water and a great view. The camp was tucked out of sight with a short walk to look down on a big meadow located just below camp. The trail that headed up the valley to the Continental Divide, paralleling the stream was about 100 yards from camp. That evening after our meal we worked our way through the timber to have a view of the meadow, there were some cow elk and calves grazing there. The next morning after a good breakfast, clean up, and bear proofing (Yep, Cutthroat country is often Bear country) the camp, we headed out to find wild trout. We picked up the trail and started working our way up the mountain, the trail had not been cleared in years, making the going slow. The elk and deer easily jumped the downed trees but it was not so easy for us bipeds. It was obvious we were going to have to find a

better way to come back to camp that afternoon. The objective for today's hike was a couple of meadows two or three miles up the valley. After climbing over blown down trees for about a mile, we decided to wade up the stream: might just as well fish while we make our way to the meadows! What a great move, the fishing was great! Oh, I forgot to say the reason we did not get in the stream to begin with was all the water falls we had to climb or work our way around; oh well, it sure was pretty. At one point we were working a nice long pool with a timbered and grassed bench on each side, as I reached down to take a fish off, Willow (my dog) leaned into my leg and started growling. I looked in the direction Willow was looking; at first I did not see anything, then there was movement! It was a big lynx! (Yep, Cutthroat country is often big cat country.) The cat was not the least bit afraid of us, I told Willow to speak, the cat just looked at us with a come-on lets get it on expression on its face. We continued to work our way up the canyon, and the fishing was amazing. The fish were in good shape and good sized; some were better than seventeen inches long.

We had a good day; now it was time to work our way back to camp. Instead of trying to go back the way we had come, we climbed up the other side of the canyon and sure enough there was a much better trail headed in the right direction. After following the trail for some time we ended up across the creek from the meadow below camp. We crossed the stream, looked back to where the trail came out of the timber, and we could not see it. Probably most hikers and fishermen will miss it like we did the day before. As trails get old and hard to follow, game makes new ones, but they forget to tell the map makers. There is about four more miles of stream with two meadows above where we stopped, making for another great scouting trip in the future. The main thing to remember is:

Don't Spread Around What You Have Found, Or It Will Not Long Be Around!

Chapter Fifteen
Conservation, Deceit,
and the Responsible Angler

"An angler, sir, uses the finest tackle, and catches his fish scientifically- trout for instance – with the artificial fly, and he is mostly a quiet, well-behaved gentleman. A fisherman, sir, uses any kind of 'ooks and lines, and catches them any way; so he gets them it's all one to 'im, and he is generally a noisy fellah, sir, something like a gunner."
Dr. George Washington Bethune (1847)

With education comes responsibility. Say you find a good Brookie stream; one with little or no evidence of visits for at least this season. Now what? Besides the obvious pleasure you take from carefully fishing this little gem, of course. Imagine what happens over the next few weeks if you accurately describe it to the fellow that runs the local fly shop. Or you talk about it at your favorite watering hole. Get it? The fact is you now have the responsibility of helping keep this special stream in pristine condition. "Why me?" you say. We say, "Who else?" The local Game Warden? Your Mother? The authors ('cause we told you how to do it)? If you don't understand this point on the ethical compass, please immediately return this book to the authors for a full refund (and our sympathy).

Now, you don't have to lie about things; we would never recommend such behavior! But it is acceptable to treat the truth with respect and discretion. You are not in a courtroom; you may tell the truth without telling the whole truth. And it is okay to just keep quiet around folks who haven't demonstrated they share your respect for wild trout fishing, the wilderness, and pure strain Rio Grande Cutthroats. It's also ethically and morally acceptable to leave out essential details as you describe the stream in question. Do you share all the details about your sex life with everyone, or at the local fly shop, or even your fishing buddies??? Remember, you are not in a courtroom. Sometimes a smile is the best contribution the responsible angler can make to a conversation, especially around folks you don't know very well.

There's more to this conservation idea than simply secrecy, although that does go a long way to preserve a good stream. YOU have to be a good steward while on stream. That means if you pack anything in; pack it back out. Plus a little extra if you find it. It means making an informed judgment on whether or not to keep a few Brookies for dinner. Sometimes that helps a stream; sometimes not. It means don't screw up the banks or wade unnecessarily. It means keeping the stream as good as new.

Chapter Sixteen
A Final Word of Encouragement

"So the trout rose freely, and to some extent imperturbably, but they discriminated. To the end I was never quite sure on what success depended most on this wonderful piece of water.
Fine gut and a perfectly floated fly and exact casting must have been of use as everywhere, but these alone were not enough."
Sir Edward Grey, *Fly Fishing* (1899)

You are now, gentle reader, ready to put all your new found knowledge to use, or maybe begin (continue) wondering why you paid good money for this little book. You are indeed well armed. You know a fly in the water is better than two in the bush (See Chapter Three) and the importance of stealth (See Chapter Four). You have also been informed you must be prepared to hike to near exhaustion before fishing (See Chapter Fourteen, Where Are These Wonderful Streams) but that is not all bad, more about that later. The notion that you must hike to the point of cardiac arrest to reach a good spot to cast your fly is not shared by all your authors, be anything but ashamed if you agree.

Try not to forget as you head for the stream you may be making a memory that will last and be treasured for a lifetime; and think of how blessed you are to be able to be making the trip and that the day may become very special. If you doubt this, reflect on how you felt when, most likely with your father or grandfather and at the ripe old age of about five or six, you caught your first fish. Or remember the look on your child's/grandchild's face at that time in their life. While there is a place for it in fly fishing, try not to be totally occupied with the science of it all. There are those among us, and some quite adept at fishing, who hold to the view that often anglers over estimate the talents of the fish.

We will now let you in on a dirty little secret which, of course, you must not widely discuss (See the Chapter on Conservation and Deceit for tips on this skill). Do not despair if you feel you may not be able to apply all you've read immediately and be advised that a significant number of fish brought to net catch themselves- that's right, they become impaled on your fly through no fault of yours.

To illustrate the above, and I assure you that you will experience something akin to this sooner rather than later, you will have been fishing for about half an hour and have not even had a strike (that you are aware of). You decide to look over the flies in the expensive fly box kept in your expensive vest and see if you can spot anything you think a fish might think it would like to eat. While you are searching for this killer fly, you let your line dangle thirty feet down stream. After you have made another guess as to what a trout might like and have hung it on the patch of lamb's wool on your chest, you begin to take up your line. To your substantial surprise, there's a fish on – feels like a good one. After you've brought her to net, admired and released her, something of an ethical dilemma is presented; how are you going to recount the experience?

Before making your decision, consider this: many hold to the view that, in a fishing context anyway, honesty is an overrated virtue and didn't Dizzy Dean say "them that can lie without bragging, let'um lie?" Think about it a little. You have hiked to near exhaustion to get to your chosen location and because of that are probably alone or at least out of sight of other anglers. This fish was alive when released and who's to say this sixteen inch trout has not grown to eighteen inches by the time you tell the story? (One of your authors holds to the view that you can add two inches without bragging, see Mr. Dean, supra). Who is the worse off for describing the event as an epic battle with an eighteen inch trout after you deftly cast your fly under an overhanging branch and about two inches from a partially submerged log some forty feet upstream and above a big riffle, rather than mentioning that the fish obviously had suicidal tendencies? This will happen; we guarantee it, not to mention the countless times you will cast your fly to a riffle, lose sight of it and have a better idea of Jimmy Hoffa's present address than the location of your fly. You raise your rod and, you guessed it, fish on! If anyone is fishing close by, don't act surprised – they will think your vision is superb and you actually saw the fish take the fly. After this happens a few times (and it will!), you will begin to believe you really saw the strike – very satisfying.

Enjoy every day you are able to go fishing and remember: "The Gods do not count against man's allotted time on this earth, days spent fishing." (Inscribed on some pharaoh's tomb we are told and if it's not, it should have been!)

It is hoped that this chapter reminds you that your day at stream side can become very special. How else can we explain why a beer tastes better when enjoyed after a day fishing, and that watching a big trout come back to life and swim away upon release just may be what it's all about. (The Hokey Pokey notwithstanding.) One of your authors has, when fishing alone, been known, on those rare occasions when a really nice trout is released, to salute as the fish swims away, while hoping that one day he and the fish will meet again.

Chapter Seventeen
Where We Put It All Together

"It has always been my private conviction that any man who pits his intelligence against a fish and loses has it coming"
John Steinbeck

These ideas and suggestions are most effective when used together, in fact it's almost required. However, sometimes better skill in one area helps mitigate undeveloped skills in another. For example, a very stealthy approach can help compensate for beginning casting skills. The following list can do two things: you can see the principals of success all together and you can copy the list, as a reminder, to include in your small stream fishing kit. If things aren't going too well on your small stream, maybe a "time out" with the list can help you get back on track.

Principles of Small Stream Fishing Success

- Be mentally prepared to change your fishing habits,
- Think "Small Stream,"
- Keep your fly in or on the water,
- Be stealthy,
- Be aware of changing conditions,
- Think about where you want to cast your fly,
- Cast effectively and accurately,
- Keep up with your fly for a timely set,
- Manage your fly line for drag-free presentations,
- Keep the stream as good as new.

At this point in the book we would normally wish you good luck in your small stream fishing endeavors, but now you know you don't need to depend on it. Other fishermen will envy you; isn't that enough? Of course, you could tell them where to buy this book.

Bibliography

Behnke, Robert, *About Trout, The Best of Robert Behnke from Trout Magazine*, The Lyons Press, 2007.

Behnke, Robert J., *Trout and Salmon of North America*, The Free Press, 2002.

Brooks, Joe, *The Complete Book of Fly Fishing*, Outdoor Life, 1958.

Goddard, John & Clarke, Brian, *Understanding Trout Behavior*, The Lyons Press, 2001.

Hinshaw, Glen A., *Crusaders for Wildlife*, Western Reflections Publishing Co., 2000.

About the Authors

F. C. "Corky" Henson began fly fishing in the mid-1980s and hasn't purchased any other type fishing equipment since. He began restoring, then making, bamboo fly rods in the late 1990s and has found no better place to test them than small streams. He is a retired polymer chemist.

Robert Goodwin, an Oklahoma State University graduate with a degree in Electrical Engineering, helped bring on the world of fiber optic telecommunications. He started wilderness backpacking and fly fishing in the 1970s and, upon retirement in 2002, began guiding adventurous anglers into the Weminuche Wilderness.

Watt Murrah's love affair with fly fishing began forty-four years ago and continues to the present day. He holds B.A. and J.D. Degrees from The University of Texas at Austin.